THE
BEST
AMERICAN
POETRY
1989

◇ ◇ ◇

THE
BEST
AMERICAN
POETRY
1989

◇　◇　◇

Donald Hall, Editor

David Lehman, Series Editor

COLLIER BOOKS

MACMILLAN PUBLISHING COMPANY

NEW YORK

Collier Books
Macmillan Publishing Company
866 Third Avenue, New York, N.Y. 10022
Collier Macmillan Canada, Inc.

ISBN 0-02-044182-7
ISSN 1040-5763

Macmillan books are available at special discounts for bulk purchases
for sales promotions, premiums, fund-raising, or educational use.
For details, contact:
Special Sales Director
Macmillan Publishing Company
866 Third Avenue
New York, N.Y. 10022

10 9 8 7 6 5 4 3 2 1

Printed in the United States of America

CONTENTS

DAVID LEHMAN *was born in New York City in 1948. His books include two poetry collections:* An Alternative to Speech *(Princeton University Press, 1986) and the forthcoming* Operation Memory *(Princeton, 1990). He is the author of a study of detective novels,* The Perfect Murder *(The Free Press, 1989), and the editor of* Ecstatic Occasions, Expedient Forms: 65 Leading Contemporary Poets Select and Comment on Their Poems *(Collier Books, 1988). He received a grant from the National Endowment for the Arts in 1987 and a Guggenheim Fellowship in poetry for 1989–90. A vice president of the National Book Critics Circle, he lives with his wife and son in Ithaca, New York.*

FOREWORD

by David Lehman

◊   ◊   ◊

A little while ago in Ithaca, New York, the university town where I live, two good bookstores decided to merge and relocate. With some fanfare, after inevitable delays, the new store opened. I headed straight for the poetry section. It was impressive: an alcove with tall bookcases on facing walls. There were easily twice as many shelves as at either of the former locations. There was only one problem. Something was wrong with the lighting system, making it difficult to read the titles on the spines of the books.

That seems an apt metaphor for the condition of contemporary poetry. There's plenty of it, and plenty of it is good, but it seems to be located in an unlit alcove where bookstore patrons fear to tread. Everyone who loves poetry must sometimes wonder whether it will languish for lack of a light bulb. An optimist, of course, would phrase that differently. An optimist would say: Our poets operate in the dark, like sure-footed jewel thieves. The wonder is that the incandescence around them is so bright.

The Best American Poetry is a publishing experiment conducted in the spirit of a wager. The experiment is to see whether a single annual volume can accurately reflect the diversity of American poetry—can reflect it with enthusiasm but also with the need to make critical discriminations—and honor excellence regardless of what form it takes, or what idiom it favors, or from which region of the country it comes. The wager is over the question of poetry's audience. Everyone complains that poetry doesn't have one. We bet the opposite—that there are more than enough readers around who would seriously like to know what the poets in America are up to these days.

The rules of this anthology series are few and flexible. Each January a different guest editor, a poet of distinguished stature, makes the selections based on works published in the previous calendar year. No volume in the series will have fewer than fifty poems or more than seventy-five; there is a limit of three poems by an individual poet in any given year; the guest editor is asked to include a poem of his or her own. The series editor is expected to support and assist the guest editor, in part by scanning the world of magazines and making preliminary recommendations. Translations are ineligible, but prose poems are as welcome as playful pantoums, "avant-garde plays," narratives, elegies, exotic formal arrangements, erotic lyrics, musings on taboo subjects, satire, "cinematic" poems, and blank verse—all of which the reader will find in the pages that follow.

Last year *The Best American Poetry* made its debut, with John Ashbery serving as guest editor. The response to that volume has been exhilarating. Appreciative reviewers noted Mr. Ashbery's ecumenical spirit. As he put it in his introduction to the volume, "I like things that seem to me good of their kind, and don't especially care what the kind is." He chose seventy-five poems by as many poets; Donald Hall, guest editor of the 1989 volume, has elected to follow suit and has done so with equal generosity and savvy. Mr. Hall is an indefatigable correspondent, and I know I will miss the frequent exchanges between us as we shipped each other poems, compared judgments, and traded ardors and bêtes noires during the six-month period in which a hill of photocopies evolved inexorably into *The Best American Poetry, 1989*. By a happy coincidence, Donald Hall was working on the anthology at the time he published *The One Day*, which won him the National Book Critics Circle prize for poetry this year—and which may be, as Olympians are taught to say, his "personal best."

Critics periodically take swipes at poetry—not at specific poets or movements but at American poetry itself, as though it were monolithic (when in fact it is diverse) and moribund (when in fact it is vital). "Contemporary poetry in the United States flourishes in a vacuum," writes one such essayist. It is possible to assent to this broad thesis—*flourishes* is the right word—without reaching the dire conclusion that poetry is finished. Consider the number, the quality, and the range of magazines that publish poetry—not grudgingly, not out of obligation, but with pleasure and conviction. Nearly three dozen are represented in *The Best American Poetry, 1989*, ranging from *The New Yorker* to *The Reaper*, from *Boulevard* to *Grand Street*, from flamboyant gadflies like *Exquisite Corpse* to classy campus-based quarterlies like *The Gettysburg Review*, not to mention the quarterly reviews with states in their names, Ohio and Iowa, Michigan and Georgia.

Yet it would be foolish to deny that poetry in America today has its share of problems. One vexing matter is the vacuum of genuine critical response. Many brainy assistant professors and graduate students, from whose ranks critics of poetry used to emerge, prefer the autotelic world of critical theory: criticism without an object outside of itself. I wish we could get these potential readers to see what they're missing. Not all but many critical theorists regard the making of evaluative aesthetic judgments as either beside the point or as downright pernicious. Given this dismal state of academic affairs, poets may have little choice but to act as their own critics, and to try to create the taste by which their works will be enjoyed. The expanded section of contributors' notes in *The Best American Poetry* is a modest step in this direction. The poets were encouraged to comment on their work, and the majority of them did so, helping us see how poems get written.

"Poetry is a pheasant disappearing in the brush," wrote Wallace Stevens. But it is also, he wrote, "a search for the inexplicable," "a renovation of experience," and "a purging of the world's poverty and change and evil and death." Critical neglect cannot defeat the impulse to make something imperishable out of the transitory words of our days.

DONALD HALL *was born in New Haven, Connecticut, in 1928. He graduated from Harvard University in 1951, studied at Oxford, and taught English at the University of Michigan from 1957 until 1975. Since then he has been a free-lance writer of poetry, criticism, sports journalism, biography, college textbooks, essays about the country, and plays. Hall's recent books include* The Ideal Bakery, *a collection of short stories (North Point Press, 1987), and* The One Day: A Poem in Three Parts, *which won the National Book Critics Circle Award for poetry in 1989 (Ticknor & Fields, 1988). He has edited* Contemporary American Poetry *(Penguin, 1972) and* The Oxford Book of American Literary Anecdotes *(Oxford, 1981). Twice awarded a Guggenheim Fellowship, he received the Lenore Marshall/Nation Poetry Prize for* The Happy Man *(Random House, 1986).*

INTRODUCTION

by Donald Hall

◊ ◊ ◊

1. Poetry in Public

Some days, when you read the paper, it seems clear that the United States is a country *devoted* to poetry. You can delude yourself reading the sports page. After finding two references to "poetry in motion," apropos figure skating and the Kentucky Derby, you read that a shortstop is the poet of his position, and that sailboats raced under blue skies that were sheer poetry. On the funny page Zippy praises Zerbina's outfit: "You're a *poem* in polyester." A funeral director, in an advertisement, muses on the necessity for poetry in our daily lives. It's hard to figure out just what he's talking about, but it becomes clear that this *poetry* has nothing to do with *poems*; it sounds more like taking naps.

Poetry, then, appears to be:

1) a vacuous synonym for excellence or unconsciousness. What else is common to the public perception of poetry?

2) It is universally agreed that no one reads it.

3) It is universally agreed that the non-reading of poetry is a. contemporary and b. progressive. From a. it follows that, some time back (a wandering date, like "olden times" for a six-year-old), our ancestors read poems, and poets were rich and famous. From b. it follows that every year fewer people read poems (or buy books or go to poetry readings) than the year before.

Other pieces of common knowledge:

4) Only poets read poetry.

5) Poets themselves are to blame because "poetry has lost its audience."

6) For that matter, everybody today knows that poetry is "useless and completely out of date"—as Flaubert's Bouvard and Pecouchet put it a century ago.

For expansion on and repetition of these well-known facts, look in volumes of *Time* magazine, in Edmund Wilson's "Is Verse a Dying Technique?," in current newspapers everywhere, in interviews with publishers, in book reviews by poets, and in the August 1988 issue of *Commentary*, where an essayist has assembled every cliché about poetry, common for two centuries, under the title "Who Killed Poetry?"

Time magazine, which reported *The Waste Land* as a hoax in 1922, canonized Eliot in a cover story in 1950. Doubtless *Time*'s writers and editors altered over thirty years, but they also stayed the same: Always the Giants grow old and die, leaving Pygmies behind. After the age of Eliot, Frost, Stevens, Moore, and Williams, the wee survivors were Lowell, Berryman, Jarrell, and Bishop. When the survivors died, younger elegiac journalists revealed that the dead Pygmies had been Giants all along—and *now* the young poets were dwarves. Doubtless obituaries lauding Allen Ginsberg are already written; does anyone remember *Life* on the Beat Generation, thirty years ago?

2. Death by Murder

"Is Verse a Dying Technique?" Edmund Wilson answered *yes* in 1928. It is not one of the maestro's better essays. Wilson's long view makes the point that doctors and physicists no longer write poetry when they contribute to their fields. Yes, Lucretius is dead. And, yes, Coleridge had a notion of poetry rather different from Horace's. But Wilson announced in 1928 that poetry had collapsed because ". . . since the Sandburg-Pound generation, a new development in verse has taken place. The sharpness and energy disappear; the beat gives way to a demoralized weakness." He speaks, of course, in the heyday of Moore and Williams, Frost, H.D., Stevens, and Eliot; in 1948 he added a paragraph nervously acknowledging Auden, whom he had put down twenty years before. He goes on, amazingly, to explain the problem's source: "The trouble is that no verse technique is more obsolete today than blank verse. The old iambic pentameters have no longer any relation whatever to the tempo and language of our lives. Yeats was the last who could write them." But Yeats wrote *no* blank verse of real interest; as it happens, two Americans of Wilson's time wrote superb blank verse. Frost starting from Wordsworth made an idiomatic American blank verse, especially in his dramatic monologues, possibly the best modern example of that measure; Stevens starting from Tennyson made blank verse as gorgeous as "Tithonus." Read Frost's "Home Burial" and Stevens's "Sunday Morning" and then tell me that blank verse was obsolete in 1928. Had Wilson not been so eager to announce poetry's demise, his intelligence would have prevented him from embracing the facile determinism of his essay. "You cannot deal with contemporary events in an idiom already growing trite in Tennyson's and Arnold's day." As it happens, the first critics to claim that iambic was "completely out of date" wrote in the eighteenth century.

Poetry was never Wilson's strong suit. It is worthwhile to remember that Wilson found Edna St. Vincent Millay the great poet of her age—better than Robert Frost, Marianne Moore, T. S. Eliot, Ezra Pound, Wallace Stevens, and William Carlos Williams. In one of Wilson's late self-interviews in *The New Yorker*, he revealed that among contemporary poets only Robert Lowell was worth reading. It saves a lot of time, not needing to check out Elizabeth Bishop, John Ashbery, Galway Kinnell, Louis Simpson, Adrienne Rich, Sylvia Plath, John Berryman. . . .

Sixty years after Edmund Wilson told us that verse was dying, Joseph Epstein in *Commentary* reveals that it was murdered. Of course, Epstein's golden age—Stevens, Frost, Williams—is Wilson's time of "demoralized weakness." Everything changes and everything stays the same. Poetry was always in good shape twenty or thirty years ago; *now* it has always gone to hell. I have heard this lamentation for forty years, not only from distinguished critics and essayists, but from professors and journalists who enjoy viewing our culture with alarm. Repetition of a formula, under changed circumstances with different particulars, does not make a formulaic complaint invalid; it suggests that the formula represents something besides its surface. In asking "Who Killed Poetry," Joseph Epstein begins by insisting that he does *not* dislike it: "I was taught that poetry was itself an exalted thing." He admits his "quasi-religious language" and asserts that "it was during the 1950s that poetry last had this religious aura." Did Mr. Epstein go to school "during the 1950s"? If he attended poetry readings in 1989 with unblinkered eyes, he would watch twenty-year-olds undergoing quasi-religious emotions—one of whom, almost certainly, will write an essay in the 2020s telling the world that poetry is mouldering in its grave.

Worship is not love. People who at the age of fifty deplore the death of poetry are the same people who in their twenties were "taught to exalt it." The middle-aged poetry detractor is the student who hyperventilated at poetry readings thirty years earlier—during Wilson's "Pound-Sandburg era," or Epstein's aura-era of "T. S. Eliot and Wallace Stevens, Robert Frost and William Carlos Williams." After college many people stop reading contemporary poetry. Why not? They become involved in journalism or scholarship, essay writing or editing, brokering or solid waste; they backslide from the undergraduate Church of Poetry. Years later, glancing belatedly at the poetic scene, they tell us that poetry is dead. They left poetry; therefore they blame poetry for leaving them. Really they lament their own aging. Don't we all? But some of us do not blame the poets.

Epstein localizes his attack on two poets, unnamed but ethnically specified: "One of the two was a Hawaiian of Japanese ancestry, the other was middle-class Jewish." He speaks disparagingly of them, with his ironic mosquito-whine, and calls their poems "heavily preening, and not distinguished enough in language or subtlety of thought to be memorable." (Pure blurbtalk.) He does not quote a line by either poet he dismisses. His essay gives no evidence that he reads the contemporary poetry he denigrates.

Dubious elegies on the death of poetry shouldn't need answers, but a frequently repeated lie can turn into a fact. Epstein reports that "last year the *Los Angeles Times* announced it would no longer review books of poems." In the *Washington Post*, Jonathan Yardley referred to the same event, which never happened, and then applauded what never happened. The editor of the *Los Angeles Times Book Review* merely announced that his paper would review *fewer* books; instead, the *Review* would print a whole poem in a box every week, with a note on the poet. In the two years since instituting this policy, the *LATBR* has continued to review poetry—more than *The New York Times Book Review* has done—and in addition has printed an ongoing anthology of contemporary American verse. The *Los Angeles Times* probably pays more attention to poetry than any other newspaper in the country. Yet when they announced the new policy, poets picketed the newspaper. We poets love to parade as victims; we love the romance of alienation and insult.

3. Mere Numbers

More than a thousand poetry books appear in this country each year. More people write poetry in this country—publish it, hear it, and presumably read it—than ever before. Let us quickly and loudly admit that no poet sells like Stephen King, that poetry is not so popular as professional wrestling, and that fewer people attend poetry readings in the United States than in Soviet Russia. Snore, snore. More people read poetry now in the United States than ever did before.

Why then does almost everyone connected with poetry claim that poetry's audience has diminished? Doubtless the pursuit of failure and humiliation is part of it. There is also a source which is lovable and sweet—if unobservant: Some of us love poetry so dearly that its absence from *everybody's* life seems an outrage. Exaggerating out of foiled passion, we claim that "no one reads poems."

When I was in school in the forties there were few poetry readings; only Frost did many. If we consult biographies of Stevens and Williams, we understand that for them a poetry reading was an unusual event. Readings picked up late in the fifties, avalanched in the sixties, and continue unabated as we approach the nineties. Readings sell books. When trade publishers in 1950 issued a third book by a moderately prominent poet, they printed 750 hardbound copies, possibly a thousand. If the edition sold out in three or four years everybody was happy. The same trade publisher in 1989 would likely print the same poet in an edition of four to five thousand, hard and soft—and the book would stand a good chance of being reprinted. Recently, a dozen or more American poets have sold by the tens of thousands, at least some of their books: Rich, Bly, Ginsberg, Ashbery, Kinnell, Creeley, Snyder, Sexton, Levertov, Forché, Plath; doubtless others. Last I knew, Galway Kinnell approached fifty thousand with *The Book of Nightmares*.

It is not only the sales of books that one can adduce to support the notion that poetry's audience has grown tenfold in the last thirty years. If the poetry reading provides the largest new audience, there are also more magazines, and magazines sell more copies. In 1955, no one would have believed you if you had suggested that two or three decades hence the United States would support a poetry magazine, bimonthly and tabloid, with a circulation of twenty thousand copies, available on newsstands from coast to coast. Everybody complains about the *American Poetry Review*; few acknowledge how remarkable it is that it exists at all.

A few years back, *Publishers Weekly* printed a list of all-time trade-paperback best-sellers, beginning with *The Joy of Sex*, which sold millions, and going as low as 250,000. It happened that I read the chart shortly after learning that Lawrence Ferlinghetti's *A Coney Island of the Mind*, a trade paperback, had sold over a million copies. Because it was poetry, *PW* understood that its sales did not count. Ginsberg's *Howl* must have passed the million mark much earlier.

When I make these points, I encounter fierce resistance. No one wants to believe them. If ever I convince people that these numbers are correct, they come up with excuses: Bly sells because he's a showman; Ginsberg is notorious; Rich sells because of feminist politics. Or people assert that only poets read poetry. Do we deride music's public by claiming that it sings in the bathtub? May we not be allowed a passion for Pavarotti, even though we play the piano?

Everybody artistic *loathes* statistics. Good. In 1988 the Philip Morris Companies funded their fifth survey of "Americans and the Arts," a poll with consequent statistics done by Lou Harris. We learn that from 1984 to 1987, ninety-seven million Americans, fifty-five percent of all adults, visited an art museum, and that during the same timespan, sixty million of us attended live ballet or modern dance.

Harris surveyed not only consumption but participation: There are ninety million photographers out there, and forty million adults take part in ballet or modern dance. So how many people do you think "write stories or poems," as the Harris people put it?

(Please pause, look away from the page, and make a guess. Since hearing this figure I have asked everyone I have bumped into. Because of the way I ask, everybody guesses high. "Two hundred thousand," they say; "a million." Once someone took a deep breath and said, "Five million.")

The correct answer, ladies and gentlemen—according to the National Center of the Arts, an affiliate of Louis Harris and Associates —is forty-two million Americans. How could "Harper's Index" miss this one? Twenty-four percent of the adult population of the United States writes poems or stories, whatever we mean by that. Needless to say, the undemocratic issue of quality is never addressed. (Hugh Kenner declares that there has never been a moment when there were more than six writers "who mattered" alive.) Although I was first flabbergasted by the figures, after a moment's thought I believed them—thinking of the response to ads for "Poems Wanted," thinking of the poetry societies, the living room workshops, the creative writing classes at night in high schools, thinking especially of the several hundred MFA programs.

So why does Ferlinghetti sell *only* a million? There is a slogan on a bookmark: "People who say that they like poetry and don't buy any are a pack of cheap sons-of-bitches."

People tend to deplore numbers, like the forty-two million, on the sensible ground that these figures never count quality. But surely large numbers *may* make distant connection with quality. England, the great country of theater, is the nation of domestic mimics; and every Kent stockbroker is a scholar of accent's nuance. English living rooms provide ongoing seminars in pronunciation and every village has its drama group. I don't claim that parlor Henry Higginses and vicarage theatricals are professional or even competent; I claim that the maple tree, wishing to grow more maple trees, is prudent to shed forty-two million seeds.

Few of the forty-two million publish. Of the few who publish, ninety percent are doubtless terrible. (Shall we require capital punishment?) Because more poems than ever are written, doubtless more bad poems are written and printed. Amen.

There are failures with pseudoprofessional sources. A few years back I talked about the mass-produced McPoem (before the McEpidemic of McFormulations) as a product of the workshop, a poem identically cooked from coast to coast. Really, there may be forty-two million kinds of failure. Certainly sloppiness is epidemic. It astonishes me how many neoformalists cannot scan. (Scansion went out with *Understanding Poetry*, more than fifty years ago, when Cleanth Brooks and Robert Penn Warren confused rhythm and meter.) Surely we must blame Ezra Pound for much of this ruin, since he claimed, as everyone remembers, that "sloppiness is the test of a man's sincerity." These days, with the benefit of contemporary critical prose style, he would have spoken with more eloquence: "Incompetence privileges an individual's authenticity."

4. Pomfret's Choice

In case my jokes leave me ambiguous: I believe that American poetry survives; it even prevails. I believe that the best American poetry of our day makes a considerable literature. *Best American Poetry, 1989* cannot embody the whole argument, but *American Poetry After Lowell*—an anthology of four hundred pages limited, say, to women and men born from the 1920s through the 1940s— could collect a large body of diverse, beautiful, intelligent, moving work—and work that will endure. Mind you, it would limit itself to one one-hundredth of one percent of the poems published.

In his introduction to *Best American Poetry, 1988*, John Ashbery claimed not to be one of those who tried to keep up. He is sensible: Keeping up is impossible, a waste of spirit in th' expense of shame. Nevertheless I try; for no good reason except curiosity, every year I look into five hundred new books of poems, less than half the crop, and glance at hundreds of magazines. "Look into" and "glance" are not modesties. Too often, as I begin reading a poem, I am chagrined to discover a dead metaphor in the third line—someone cups something; something darts to its harbor which is also a shield;

something either echoes or mirrors, take your pick—and I read no further. If Roethke had cradled his meadow mouse first thing in the poem, doubtless I would never have reached the paralytic stunned in the tub; doubtless I have missed wonderful poems because of early hideous blemishes. Reading for *Best American Poetry, 1989*, I have forced myself to admit some dead metaphors, maybe even an unscannable line in a metrical poem, and certainly a disgusting line break or two—for the famous sake of the whole . . . although I have wept salt tears over my principled antinomianism.

This year I have read more magazines than ever, including magazines I had never heard of until this year. Among my seventy-five poets, I have included a dozen of whom I knew nothing a year ago. To David Lehman I owe the magazines and poets new to me. He works hard to keep up, and yet I showed him a few magazines that *he* had not heard of. Still, as we both know, we have not read half of what's out there; we must have missed good things.

Forty-two million writers—or two hundred thousand, or three hundred—make judgment difficult. The Lottery Effect takes over —for prizes, for fellowships, for book publication, and for reprinting in anthologies. The Lottery Effect occurs when numbers diminish the possibilities of judgment, allowing too much weight to chance: On what day, or at what time of day, did the editor or judge approach this book or that poem? Most critics avoid the Lottery Effect by denial, as when Edmund Wilson claimed that Robert Lowell alone was worth reading. It saves time, but it's a lie. I have no suggestions for overcoming the Lottery Effect, except to propose more lotteries.

When I was in my twenties and writing iambic stanzas, Allen Ginsberg's "Howl" was a living reproach. For a while I denigrated Allen: "If he's right, I must be wrong." Such an either/or is both silly and commonplace: Restrictions are impoverishments. In the 1930s one was not allowed to admire both T. S. Eliot and Thomas Hardy; it was difficult for intellectuals who admired Wallace Stevens and his bric-a-brac to find houseroom for Robert Frost and his subjects. Because I wish to avoid such restrictions, or in reparation of youthful error, I am afflicted by the desire to *represent* different endeavors; I mean to be eclectic. I hope that a passion for inclusiveness may be as genuine as other people's certainties of exclusion. My two favorite poets of my own generation are Geoffrey Hill and Robert Creeley. It ought to be impossible to love both—but it isn't. Thus this book prints Daniel Mark Epstein together with Elaine Equi; David Shapiro with Karl; Bob Perelman with John Hollander; David Budbill with Elizabeth Spires and Tom Clark.

The poems I selected first have mostly remained first in my heart, poems I loved the moment I saw them, often the good work of poets already cherished. Other poems grew on me until they became as ineluctable as the first. A third category *fascinated* me, poems I enjoyed despite blemishes or flaws, sometimes poems that fail but retain wonderful passages. Other matters appearing moot, I chose my final poems by my ecumenical principles. I wanted to include schools, areas, genres, and approaches; I wanted narrative, meter, California, formalism, politics, deconstruction, deep image, and Deep South. Some poems that I include with enthusiasm show old-fashioned virtues—beauty of image and vowel, memorable or singing speech. The old ways work when genius uses them. Maybe the oldest way is *story*; the new outcropping of narrative, plot's return, shows frequently among these poems. Certain other verbal assemblies here relentlessly examine themselves, engines of irony, skeptical investigations of the word. I want both extremes and all points between.

Modernism was international. Now regions turn smaller and smaller. Among the results are concepts like "the Los Angeles poem," not to mention "the New York School"; the result seems not regionalism but clubbishness, perhaps another result of numbers this time multiplied and diminished by space or place. Sources of this increasing provincialism are understandable, but results are discouraging. Because the series editor lives in the East as I do, this selection is doubtless limited by geography. American regional biases make a politics little touched upon, belittled by easterners (like WASPs asking, "*What* racial prejudice?") and best known by southerners. A *New Yorker* reviewer, talking about Robinson Jeffers, constantly modifies her nouns with "Californian." *All geographical adjectives are diminutive*—as in "midwestern sestinas" or "Oregon neoclassicists."

California envies and berates the snobbish East while dumping on the Midwest. The Northwest understands its own superiority and the willful ignorance of the rest of the country. The Midwest prides itself on its superior sincerity while it is consumed with envy east and west; that a Michigan anthology should call itself *The Third Coast* is worth weeping over. Meantime the South, with all its subdivisions, grumbles that everybody ignores it, which is true, and that it's really best, which isn't necessarily true. Of these competing provincialisms, the East's is the most provincial.

Several American poets whom I admire are absent because they published nothing in 1988 or because they did not publish their best work. The series editor declined to be included.

Certain habits inculcate humility; sleeping in a coffin and skulls for inkwells have proved useful. For a Famous Poet, should there be such, it would be instructive to attend to poets laureate like Shadwell and Austin, or to acknowledge superstars of poetry's golden age—when everybody read poetry—like Thomas Moore with *Lallah Rookh* and Mrs. Browning with *Aurora Leigh*. In general, it is useful to rummage in the past for evidences that the taste of any moment may be impermanent. In *Lives of the Poets*, Samuel Johnson remarked the most popular English poet of all time, in the nation of Shakespeare, Donne, Milton, Marvell, Dryden, and Pope: "Perhaps no composition in our language has been oftener perused than Pomfret's *Choice*."

For the editor of a volume calling itself *Best American Poetry*, a useful advisory is the dusty corridor of an indiscriminate used bookstore where he may examine volumes of the *Anthology of Magazine Verse* edited by William Stanley Braithwaite early in this century. *Verse*, of course, is more modest than *Poetry*, and *Magazine* is modest almost to the point of appropriateness. Still, it can be sobering, looking at Braithwaite's selections from the heyday of modernism, to set some poets who published in magazines that year but remained uncollected (often Pound, Eliot, Williams, Stevens, Moore, and H.D.) against the tables of contents in which Bliss Carman, Witter Bynner, Percy Mackaye, and Jessie Rittenhouse are the household names.

*   *   *

But it is useless to worry about how one's taste will look in the future. In the richest year of the language richest in the tradition of poetry, seventy-five poets have never written seventy-five poems that entered the canon a century later. *Best American Poetry, 1989* may not address itself to 2089 but to the Muse of the Moment, to whom all poems are addressed. For a reader who lives in the present, a reader open and receptive rather than grudging, the poems in this book will demonstrate the bounty of American poetry now.

THE
BEST
AMERICAN
POETRY
1989

◊ ◊ ◊

A. R. AMMONS

Anxiety's Prosody

◇ ◇ ◇

Anxiety clears meat chunks out of the stew, carrots, takes
the skimmer to floats of greasy globules and with cheesecloth

filters the broth, looking for the transparent, the colorless
essential, the unbeginning and unending of consommé: the

open anxiety breezes through thick conceits, surface congestions
(it likes metaphors deep-lying, out of sight, their airs misting

up into, lighting up consciousness, unidentifiable presences),
it distills consonance and assonance, glottal thickets, brush

clusters, it thins the rhythms, rushing into longish gaits, more
distance in less material time: it hates clots, its stump-fires

level fields: patience and calm define borders and boundaries,
hedgerows, and sharp whirls: anxiety burns instrumentation

matterless, assimilates music into motion, sketches the high
suasive turnings, mild natures tangled still in knotted clumps.

from *Poetry*

1

JOHN ASHBERY

"*Meanwhile . . .*"

◇ ◇ ◇

Meanwhile
far above
the street

the same voices keep watch

Betty and ice cubes
salesmen listing to tell their
side of the story

all is music, unfledged
still

and how prosaic the ties to
nonetheless near meanings
as we
proceed back to a gift.

Fatally the pins fall
no man or other can bore
into the diatonic request
making its demand

on us, on youth

from *Mudfish*

Northern Idylls

◇　◇　◇

During spring break Debbie Schwartz and I would bike
    from south Minneapolis to the boathouse near the U.
        The water-soaked musk of the dock, the pungence of rotting

Enveloped in fog the rowboat with its three occupants
    moves down river between stands of birch. The adolescent
        boy gazes at the tree-trunks glimmering like bodies which

When I lifted my paddle water would bead on the slender
    blade. I'd lift and ply, lift and ply,
        then backwater. A long, green leaf, the canoe would slide into

The boy is singing, dispensing notes the way
    birds do, with a sort of mindless purity, while the men,
        uniforms stiff with frost, flex their huge, red

There, the Mississippi was shallow and brown as amber.
    Taking turns, we'd paddle, then ship our oars and remove
        our shirts. In minutes our breasts would sting as if

He is singing Hungarian folksongs. At the camp, the soldiers
    discovered he could sing. They discovered his voice the way
        they discovered jewelry sewn into the lining of the clothes of

One night, in rowboats, two to a pod, we eased out onto
    Lake Calhoun, our voices like thrown matches, flaring
        and dying. Leon rowed me, his hair metaphysical, his

Though they can't understand the words, they hum the tunes.
The one with the scar thinks of Liszt. He imagines he's in Venice,
   he imagines his gondola is drifting toward the hotel where his
   lover

After Edna and I left the Rosens' dock, the wind
   came up. We were entangled in reeds. We rowed for hours,
   muscles aching, until, luckily, Squish discovered the missing

The boy's voice falters as if he has forgotten or remembered
   something. In their damp uniforms the men shiver. The boy's
   cheeks are blanched, mottled as birchbark, with the cold or

Voices raucous with insults and laughter, my father and Moishe Rosen
   argued politics, oars waving, while we kids threaded our lines
   with angleworms to hook sunfish and perch, or bullheads as
   black as

Shouting, the soldiers prod the sly-faced peasants,
   and demand eggs or newly butchered meat for the officer's table.
   They flourish their pistols while the boy drags sacks reeking of

How I loved those summers on the lakes and rivers, imagining
   I was Sacajawea or Evangeline, gliding down waterways
   or through the bayous in melancholy search for my lost

Attention! They sit up straight, they button their collars.
   Good soldiers. They will make the boy row on the way back
   upstream.
   His voice pierces the fog, while sleet scours the freshly dug

from *The Gettysburg Review*

"It Is Marvellous . . ."

◇ ◇ ◇

It is marvellous to wake up together
At the same minute; marvellous to hear
The rain begin suddenly all over the roof,
To feel the air clear
As if electricity had passed through it
From a black mesh of wires in the sky.
All over the roof the rain hisses,
And below, the light falling of kisses.

An electrical storm is coming or moving away;
It is the prickling air that wakes us up.
If lightning struck the house now, it would run
From the four blue china balls on top
Down the roof and down the rods all around us,
And we imagine dreamily
How the whole house caught in a bird-cage of lightning
Would be quite delightful rather than frightening;

And from the same simplified point of view
Of night and lying flat on one's back
All things might change equally easily,
Since always to warn us there must be these black
Electrical wires dangling. Without surprise

The world might change to something quite different,
As the air changes or the lightning comes without our blinking,
Change as our kisses are changing without our thinking.

from *American Poetry Review*

ROBERT BLY

My Father at 85

◊ ◊ ◊

His large ears hear
everything.
He listens,
and a hermit
wakes and sleeps
in the hut underneath
his gaunt cheeks.
His eyes blue,
alert,
disappointed
and suspicious
complain
I do not bring him
the nurse's jokes.
He is a small bird
waiting to
be fed,
mostly beak,
an eagle or vulture
or the Pharoah's
servant
just before death.
My arm
on the bed
rests
relaxed
with new love.

All I know
of the Troubadors
I bring
to this bed.
I do not
want or need
to be shamed
by him
any longer.
The general of shame
has dis-
charged him,
and left him
in this small
provincial Egyptian town.
If I do not
wish
to shame him,
then why
not love him?
His long
hands, large, veined,
capable, can
still retain
or hold what he wants.
But is that
what he desired?
Some powerful
engine of desire
keeps on running
inside him.
He never phrased
what he desired,
and I
am his son.

from *Common Ground*

8

Twins of a Gazelle Which Feed Among the Lilies

◊ ◊ ◊

Antlers butting against the full moon.
Bellies lolling on my belly.

Creamy chestnut crania in convex cones.
Dogs they follow me around in circles.

Everything I do they mimic. When I laugh they laugh,
    when I cry they howl.
Fins breakwater, slice the waves that make up my body.

Galactopoietic forms that feed the Milky Way.
Hunchbacks girdled to the chest for life.

Interwoven compartments of lobules containing a network
    of tubes.
Joined to the tubes of each lobe are ducts and all ducts lead
    to the nipple.

Knots for tongues to untie.
Lazy-boy recliners for lips to sit on.

Mushroom explosions taped to the chest.
Naked reminders of the death cup cloud.

O mammilla O
Papilla.

Quivering wolf snouts nose through my dreams.
Rats on a whiskered basso-relievo.

Sleep on your back they point to the stars.
Two points earned at birth. Nightpoints to stick to a
  crying baby.

U × 2.
Vaulted cupola. Baldheaded misers hoarding the mammon.

Women lie topless, side by side on the beach, from A-flat to
  C-sharp to 3-D.
Xylophones for the sun to play on.

Yes, to say, Yes
Zeugma. Zucchetto. Zoo.

from *The Paris Review*

Of the Knowledge of Good and Evil

◇ ◇ ◇

Perhaps in the dead of some different night,
Staring into an ocean of as yet unnamed stars
About whose myriad formations we can only surmise;
Perhaps in the heat of a meridional afternoon,
Sprawled beside a water hole in the lush shade
Afforded by primitive plants, lazily swatting flies;
Or perhaps while smeared with grease from the carcass,
Having gorged at long last on a feast of raw flesh,
Listening contentedly to the sounds of digestion—
Into what immense mind on what terrible occasion
Did that thought, that first idea, finally arrive?
Salve homo, I see you there, struck by your sapience,
Stunned by the source of all bitterness and joy,
Conceiving behind wild eyes and a thickset brow
The origin of so much beauty, of so many misdeeds,
Of every identical dread: the origin of the species.
Somewhere great clouds of insects must be swarming,
For you hear their furious humming fill the air;
Somewhere a taloned beast must be tearing its prey,
For you scent the sweet odor of blood on the breeze.
You with the hairy belly, with the heavy jaw ajar,
I see you there, your mind leaping to conclusions:
The cold sweat bursts forth and you twirl a twig,
Idly, abstractedly, envisioning so many things
(Stones piled on each other, bones heaped in a pit),

Imagining every end, getting it all in an instant,
The dissolution of that time and place, of you,
Its mockeries and implication.

from *The New Yorker*

What I Heard at the Discount Department Store

◊   ◊   ◊

Don't touch that. And stop your whining too.
Stop it. I mean it. You know I do.
If you don't stop, I'll give you fucking something
to cry about right here
and don't you think I won't either.

So she did. She slapped him across the face.
And you could hear the snap of flesh against the flesh
halfway across the store. Then he wasn't whining anymore.
Instead, he wept. His little body heaved and shivered and wept
He was seven or eight. She was maybe thirty.
Above her left breast, the pin said: Nurse's Aide.

Now they walk hand in hand down the aisle
between the tables piled with tennis shoes
and underpants and plastic bags of socks.

I told you I would. You knew I would.
You can't get away with shit like that with me,
you know you can't.
You're not in school anymore.
You're with your mother now.
You can get away with fucking murder there,
but you can't get away with shit like that with me.

Stop that crying now I say
or I'll give you another little something
like I did before.

Stop that now. You'd better stop.

That's better. That's a whole lot better.
You know you can't do that with me.
You're with your mother now.

from *Longhouse*

Hotel Tropicana

◊ ◊ ◊

It wasn't hysterical it was enigmatic:
John asks the students if any of them believed
in ghosts, or spirits. No one said a word.
One shook his head slightly, no, no one else
shook anything at all.

I told a committee at an interview that poetry
could be a kind of stuttering. They lowered their heads in unison,
I lost the job. I believe
I would have lost the job anyway
but maybe my wife would have stood a chance.

Outside/within American and I assume cities of the world
there are Peep Shows, Adult Worlds. Often
they are within firing range of a bus station, a train stop.
Often.

I am in love with the world tonight for I was sincere
when I threw my body against his to protect him in the bar
from what I feared
were gunshots. They were firecrackers, it was the 4th of July
in the Year of the Tall Ships, I had forgotten.
The bar was too empty to laugh.

There is a generous fire in my friend.
And he kept two finches and did not want them to die.
Of course when he was younger . . . like me in that anything could

die and it didn't matter, it did not die. If you went
to public school you would go to hell
but you would not die.

John's uncle, whose name I've misplaced: if anyone complimented
          his attire
he said something like "You like these shoes?
These shoes cost me fifty dollars."

from *Epoch*

AMY CLAMPITT

A Minor Tremor

◊ ◊ ◊

Lunch hour in flowery,
eucalypt-boled Berkeley:
a spume off the Pacific
just scathed the easy-going sun
as equilibrium
on surreptitious horseback

bucked, dipped, swung
like a censer. A minor
tremor, said the habitué.
I looked about me
with no alarm.
We had been talking

of Milton, I remember.
The oracles are dumb;
with hollow shriek the steep
(he wrote) *of Delphos leaving.*
Not so. The unbroken broncoes
of Horse Poseidon

are the least of it. Moloch
is back, a still bigger spender.
Frenzy's a drugstore commodity.

The lost sheep feast daily
on the scaly horror
with Perrier and french fries.

from *Boulevard*

For Robert Duncan

◊   ◊   ◊

d. February 3, 1988

How the arm moved
throwing the poet's
ashes out of the boat
how it all comes back

How the whole story
form of telling curves
the story around
these cosmic corners

How the stars swam
how the moon
was dying down
out over the water

To loosen out into
those big quiet waters
little pieces of
us all are floating on

from *Exquisite Corpse*

Paris . . .

◇   ◇   ◇

Standing just outside the brass linings of Paris . . .
Beginnings that stop with jolts, like
this trip to Paris . . .
It seemed like a new life
and now it's gone.

•

And then they all just go back to their lives.
But I don't have a life. I have
this inestimable work.

•

What you don't see
is what comes through without.
The several lives . . .
contained in one the several lives . . .
But the greetings and the lastings, that's what is wanted.

•

The richness of the scene is the complete.
Avenues. You never really knew avenues
until here. They curve.

•

There are three things, and then five, and then
more. Many. Something else goes by them.
Things are settled and do not ever move.
Again.

·

Looking down from the four stories,
I see the movements, them in the street.
A corner past. The lives that meet,
that go past and do not. Skirts.
No breeze. Morning shine on the gray
curved tops. Pigeons and bells.

·

I wanted to write about Paris, but
it was a life I had left. A music
I was not to hear. The memory is in
the rhythm of the light. A rhythm never
singular. A spreading I cannot approach
and knock.

·

Time is of groups. Friends. New ones.
We go to a place together. We are never
left. Big roaring gangs in cafes with
the midst of other roaring gangs.
Godard films it all as if combined,
mirrored into a single side angle.
It's impossible to recall the speech
of the drinking.

·

Do you want to have these cigarettes?
Who has them now?

·

Bright avenue, I worship you. I have
brought this far into the extended world.
A chain of command. It has a life
which is out, onto the streets. No division
so spoken as a wish. I walk in the place.
I have walked there. I see it all.
I no longer quite see it. I have been.
I am one.

·

The longer you think, the fuller you stop.
The wisher you want to be you. I sit by you.
We walk by. The windows throw gold.
The sun is in team. Remarks, as if chosen,
unchosen. The three more you will meet.
We. Going together. Witnessed en masse.
A small case in a museum contains all
his roses.

·

They were liars and embraced. They told the
wanted tales. Night always and failure and
the things. The things waiting to be remembered
undone. A facade. The movie was playing.
Another facade. The black suits arriving
in the buses in the night.

·

Complementary and shivered. The books
of avail in the white store. Mallarmé.
And the exiles. A bird landing, then another one.
The information at the same times of night.
Groups around, listening, commenting. More
drinks and only then more work.

·

She lived near the spray of waters.
The long boulevard of quells. The grand
boulevard of closeness having doubts. A
handsome and useless gate. He ate often in
this restaurant. The one of the sea-green light
and women transparent to the ceiling.

.

Where we hid and talked and made light.
Made time. The place of memory is the one
unknown before. I take your cigarette
and thank you. I thank the world
in small for its roll.

.

It's short, Paris. And large, function.
The pencil will reach every corner.
Every opal glass grape halfway to the ceiling.
When we pigged out on pig, and observed the
level voice of the petit bourgeois increase
with the meal. So much warm light caught
we did not notice the destruction outside
anymore.

.

A calming careful reciting of menus.

.

Everyone must know. Everyone must stay,
but they go. Everyone's lives, street by street.
Does he live over the sign that says . . . ?
When it turns on a phrase. Where it lives
by the shine of the committed phone.

.

A certain weightless facet, Paris.

.

In the quick window (we do not go in)
the huge poster of Le Mépris. And it is all
big Bardot in Yellow. And besides it's
normal.

•

Life in its endless crystallization going in.

•

Will you have more of the vodka
of an amber Russian basement
chilled in carafe preceding
the reading and with buffalo grass?

•

Then the night again, and restaurants, and
tobacco afloat of a zincish hue.
How the conversation was vast, and the light
of your eyes an inroad beyond all
perimeters of the former life.

•

How you dream in Paris the dream that
makes up your day.

•

Fast embracing eyes and talking the words out.

•

You go through all of it. It might have been
you going through it. Long ago on the walls
of last week. And the tiniest crack or
abrade there was drawn by someone.

•

You walked out ahead of me fast. But
I was faster and I caught the door.
It was the car and we were going somewhere, to
be taken somewhere again. Where there

———
24

would be no music. The parties had no music.
Poets. Food. Drinks. Smokes. Talk in bunches.
The bland dark sheets of her paintings on the
walls were the walls. Not so good, someone said.
Sometimes laughter and tales told again of the
older poetry times. A black cat passes through.
We are in his apartment, it is a place of halls
and it is late. We go out through the unlit
garbage can passage, the street out there.
But the thought comes that there is no
return to any of this.

•

We love each other and have never spoken.

•

You think you know what it is?
Green grass. White cobbles. Waiting.
I cannot write. My hand grows weak.
I continue. Not cobbles. Gravel.
At the side of the museum at the appointed
time but they do not come. My hand
grows wavy. Wary? Don't forget to dot
the importance of a mistake. How I came
to be here. There. After the appropriate
fifteen minutes I went away. But I
had seen.

•

The pictures were all quite visible, though
none intensely lit. The sensation that
true paint should glow from beneath
once given just enough light for a start.
What of those Monets certainly painted
outdoors in full sun? They had soaked up so much
light that day that surely they were still giving it
back? Perhaps I should have waited
a bit longer for them to come?

•

Why am I writing this? For no reason
in the world. This kind of writing is a sort
of waiting. For the true writing to come,
the words that will have soaked up
enough . . . what? Late, and I have
not even one fire to put out. The sentences
all on strips of paper like hat bands and spin.

•

To be given the gleam of a new life
and then be hurled away from the crack.
Abysmal. Melville (Ishmael) had accepted
the exile's life of writer. He stood
with his back to the city's edge and faced the
water of that first page. What we (I)
want is formless. A single pronoun is
never enough. The lights come on in the life
and there are always many. As if a
phantom "too" accompanied each sentence.
Have I not copied myself sufficiently?
Standing below the granite sheer and watching
its darkest blue edge. My pen will
never reach.

•

Once you realize that each word has a life
of sizeless shifts of meaning . . .

•

The leaves have grown again to cover
the times to see. Even in the dark
the lights will not show.

•

My word "and" in my quick hand
has become a drawing of no meaning.
Or little. Or there is still something I
could invent to fit it. I woke up
with it once beneath my hand.

．

I keep trying to sketch the person, myself.
There is still sometimes a resonance in
the house of the phone bell we no longer have.
That invention is larger than we thought.
And sometimes I think I have more
words than are possible.

．

Drop it, whatever thing you had hoped to
cling to. Drop it down your life.

．

A fine clutter there. Sterling inventions
in careless treatment. A hole in a noun.
A mouse on fire. The whole hoop of
intention revealing flaws in the exterior
as it spins. Away down the sky before
dawn the roaring plane has become an
empty bottle.

．

The handsome and useless gate of André Breton.

．

I see the monuments.
I near the rest of my life.
I take what's left of Picasso's hand.

from *O.blēk*

True Solar Holiday

◇ ◇ ◇

Out of the whim of data,
Out of binary contests driven and stored,
By the law of large numbers and subject to that law
Which in time will correct us like an event,
And from bounce and toss of things that aren't even things,
I've determined the trend I call "you" and know you are real,
Your unwillingness to appear
In all but the least likely worlds, as in this world
Here. In spite of excursions, despite my expenditures
Ever more anxiously matrixed, ever baroque,
I can prove we have met and I've proved we can do it again
By each error I make where otherwise one couldn't be
Because only an actual randomness
Never admits a mistake. It's for your sake,
Then (*though the stars get lost from the bottle,*
Though the bottle unwind), if I linger around in the wrong
Ringing up details, pixel by high bit by bit,
In hopes of you not as integer but at least as the sum
Of all my near misses, divisible,
Once there is time, to an average that poses you perfectly
Like a surprise, unaccidentally credible
Perfectly like a surprise. Am I really too patient
When this is the only program from which you derive?
Not if you knew how beautiful you will be,
How important it is your discovery dawn on me,
How as long as I keep my attention trained
Then finally the days

Will bow every morning in your direction
As they do to the sun that hosannas upon that horizon
Of which I am witness and not the one farther on:
Set to let me elect you as if there were no other choice,
Choice made like temperature, trend I can actually feel.

from *The Yale Review*

Age

◊ ◊ ◊

Most explicit—
the sense of trap

as a narrowing
cone one's got

stuck into and
any movement

forward simply
wedges one more—

but where
or quite when,

even with whom,
since now there is no one

quite with you— Quite? Quiet?
English expression: *Quait?*

Language of singular
impedance? A dance? An

involuntary gesture to
others *not* there? What's

wrong here? How
reach out to the

other side all
others live on as

now you see the
two doctors, behind

you, in mind's eye,
probe into your anus,

or ass, or bottom,
behind you, the roto-

rooter-like device
sees all up, concludes

"like a worn out inner tube,"
"old," prose prolapsed, person's

problems won't do, must
cut into, cut out . . .

The world is a round but
diminishing ball, a spherical

ice cube, a dusty
joke, a fading,

faint echo of its
former self but remembers,

sometimes, its past, sees
friends, places, reflections,

talks to itself in a fond,
judgmental murmur,

alone at last.
I stood so close

to you I could have
reached out and

touched you just
as you turned

over and began to
snore not unattractively,

no, never less than
attractively, my love,

my love—but in this
curiously glowing dark, this

finite emptiness, *you, you, you*
are crucial, hear the

whimpering back of
the talk, the approaching

fears when I may
cease to be me, all

lost or rather lumped
here in a retrograded,

dislocating, imploding
self, a uselessness

talks, even if finally to no one,
talks and talks.

from *New American Writing*

Letter from the Poetry Editor

◇ ◇ ◇

I write you this because, to your surprise
perhaps, I have grazed through your poems
as a chance visitor to your room might, noting
a pair of green slippers dropped beside the bed
and a half-finished letter on the desk—
which I have read. From such clues I can guess
that you allowed yourself to be interrupted,
and why you walked outside, and where. I know
something about your habits, how you touch
the words you choose, which edges you have crimped,
those which you've not been able to unbalance.
I know more than you want me to, perhaps,
about what you are obsessed by, whether you
have ravished your desire or been flung back;
I've read the sayings that you call your own,
the ways you take to try to make them ours.

You might not think that you were spied upon,
but take my word, at least, that I was here
when you were out. And found you in, at home.

from *The New Criterion*

DAVID DOOLEY

The Reading

◊ ◊ ◊

You see auras, do you not? No? You will,
and very soon. I could tell when you came in,
you were using your psychic, trying to figure out
what this old gal was up to. And that's good!
Just settle back in that armchair, put your feet up,
the gizmo is there on the side, honey, and I'll sit down here
in my special chair. As many times as I've sat here to give a reading,
this chair must be more psychic than most so-called fortune tellers.
Close your eyes if it helps. Your aura is lovely,
I see the purple and the silver-white and the healing green,
but there is a lime green you need to get rid of.
You are truly, in the deepest sense, a beautiful soul.
You have a highly spiritual nature, you want to
float on the mystery of life like a boat on a still lagoon.
For you the mind, and you have a good mind, is not enough,
you want to press beyond the veils. Now I know
there'll be questions you want to ask, but just hang on,
I may give you the answer before you ask the question!
That big one, the question you're dying to ask,
the answer is no. I don't hold out any hope.
Now when I say you have a spiritual nature,
and I truly believe you may have a mission
as one of the forerunners of the New Age, I don't mean to suggest
you don't care what's going on on this planet,
because you most definitely do, and furthermore, you are a,
how shall I say this, a very healthy woman. And your husband,
you're not wearing a ring, it's in your purse tied up in a handkerchief,

well, your all's romantic fires don't burn as brightly
as they once did. And this other man you wanted to ask me about,
oh, a beautiful soul, I can't see his eyes or hair,
kind of skinny-like, a beautiful, magnanimous soul,
but nothing but trouble for you. He's not a redhead.
There's already been one redheaded man in your life,
and that was enough. My first husband was redheaded,
and one day he up and de-camped with a blonde but brown
        at the roots
divorcee from down the street, and me with six kids.
This man you're so crazy about, he won't ever leave his wife.
Now I'm not one to speak out against romance, but you can't
live in fairyland all your life, so wake up, Cinderella,
and get out of that pumpkin! Your children—three of them?
two boys, isn't it—that youngest one's a real scamp,
I can see that grin of his. He leads a charmed life,
the girls are going to be all over him. Just remember
to be firm with him, he needs it, and the oldest boy,
different as day and night. You shouldn't worry about him,
he's serious and takes things hard, but he'll come through.
Solid. Rock solid. He won't tell you how much you mean to him,
but you'll know. That daughter of yours, what can we say about her?
She's just like you, only even more stubborn, she's a rebel
the way you never were. I can see her as a little girl,
stomping that foot up and down, "I won't do it!
I won't do it!"—doesn't matter what.
Let me soothe your mind about one thing, I don't see
anything bad happening to her. Oh, sorrow and unhappiness,
yes Lord, plenty of that, but nothing bad. She's got a nose
that can smell out any man that's wrong for her
no matter where he's hiding. Let her go her own way,
since she will regardless, love her when you can,
and if she starts throwing things, don't forget to duck!
Your husband's a good man, you have to provoke him
to get mad, just so you can get mad at him,
I can see you off in the corner sulking up a storm.
The two of you are not soulmates, your soulmate
did not take earthly shape during this incarnation,

but wait till the lifetime after next! My new husband
and I are soulmates, but why did he wait to show up
till I was fat and fifty? Everything happens for a purpose,
that's what I've always known in my bones, and that's what
my guides tell me. Your husband will never understand you,
but he loves you. You're the only poetry he's ever known.
What lies ahead for you two isn't clear to me, though I don't see
any major changes in your life anytime soon. I'm sorry,
I know that's not the answer you wanted. One thing I do see
is your interest in the spiritual becoming greater and greater,
and if you feel the need to meet with like-minded souls,
the study group meets right here every Thursday at seven.
Whew! I don't see another thing. Every time after one of these
I feel like I've been rode hard and put away wet.
There's coffee on the stove, and this cigarette, if I can light it,
is going to taste mighty good. And remember this, dear,
the ones in the shining robes never fail to provide light.
Have a cinnamon roll with your coffee—homemade.
I feel the need for a taste of sweet when I come back down.

from *The Volcano Inside*

RITA DOVE

The Late Notebooks
of Albrecht Dürer

◊ ◊ ◊

Every face in Nürnberg is beautiful,
but what makes one lovelier than all the others?
And the body—should the breasts be full or piquant?
How much imperfection forestalls boredom—
could it be measured in degrees?

The winter alleys reek of killed meat.
Inside, warmed inkwell, dry pepper of parchment
and the resinous disclosure of ink,
crosshatchings repeated ever fainter until
they blur, shadows on a baby's scalp
becoming a parakeet's nervous
self-admiration.

What is it one *admires* in a wife?
What was it set the Negress
beyond definition?

For there is no fair person alive on this earth
who could not be fairer.

───────────

What follows is a description of how to draw a man
eight heads tall, and it is as follows:

Item: from the skull to the soles is one unit. (The man
is standing with legs apart.)
>*From the skull to under the chin is ⅛.*
>*From under the chin to the end of the forehead is ⅟₁₀.*
>*This tenth is to be divided by two points*
>*Into three equal fields:*
>*The lowest field is inhabited by mouth and chin.*
>*In the next the nose and ears.*
>*In the third the forehead.*
And in the top fourth of the field the head begins
To curve.

A perfectly nice woman enters the room,
offering the saint some words of advice
while the devil blows evil thoughts into his ear
by means of a bellows. The woman
is ordinary and has covered her nakedness.
The saint appears to be sleeping.
Cupid, preoccupied, is trying on stilts.

The daisy is the eye of God.
Laurel is immortality.
Myrtle equals peace and love.
Pansy is Virgin, remembrance & reflection.
Primroses are St. Peter's keys.

The white rose, purity.
The red, martyrdom.
Yellow, impossible perfection
and papal benediction.

The fig is lust.
The gourd, resurrection.

Carnations sprang up from Mary's tears
on her way to Calvary,
masked the vinegar stench
with the scent of clove, too sweet
not to sicken
at the sight of a nail
driven into those magical feet.

And this carnation is the flower
of pure love, of marriage and mothers.
And the pomegranate cracks
from the pressure of its own juice,
spilling seed everywhere. And
the columbine waits. And the bluebell
surprises. And the anemone teaches

to forget the bright surface,
to unclench and go down where love leads us.

———————

But beauty is nevertheless created by human beings,
and the judgment therein so doubtful,
that we can find two persons, both
quite beautiful and charming, and yet neither
resembles the other in a single part or portion—
neither in measure nor type. Nor do we understand
which is lovelier, so blind is our comprehension.

———————

Landscape with Dairy Cottage

The appreciation of countryside is reserved for those
not participating in it—i.e., for the observer,
the traveller resting between points.
So if, by quirk, a milkmaid returning
with a basket of eggs stops to
look, it is with embarrassment
at being sidetracked from essential chores.
When, however, an entire people

enjoys the landscape in which they exist
& praises it excessively in song & rhyme—
this is highly suspicious
of that taint of character
known as nationalism,
which is nothing more
than the sin of pride transferred
to something outside the individual
over which he or she has no control . . .
& therefore no right to claim.

from *The Gettysburg Review*

STEPHEN DUNN

Letting the Puma Go

◊　◊　◊

I'll make a perfect body, said God,
and invent ways to make it fail.
Lines removed from the poem

He liked to watch the big cats.
He liked their beautiful contempt,
yet imagined how they might change
and love him
and stretch out near his feet
if he were to let them go.
And of course he wanted
to let them go
as he wanted to let himself go,
grateful for the iron bars, the lock.
He'd heard the tiger succeeds
only once in twenty hunts—
the fragile are that attuned
and that fast—
and was confused again about God,
the god who presided here.
He'd watch the tigers at feeding time,
then turn to the black panther,
its languid fierce pacing, and know
it was possible not to care
if the handsome get everything.
Except for the lions.
Hadn't the lions over the years

become their names, like the famous?
But he could spend half an afternoon
with those outfielders,
the pumas, cheetahs, leopards.
So this is excellence, he imagined:
movement toward the barely possible,
the puma's dream
of running down a hummingbird
on a grassy plain.
And then he'd let the puma go;
just before closing time
he'd wish-open its cage
and follow it into the suddenly
uncalm streets,
telling all the children it was his.

from *Poetry*

RUSSELL EDSON

The Rabbit Story

◇   ◇   ◇

A man with a broken rabbit . . .

Of it he said, broke his ears and whiskers being born. Once grew a beautiful set of teeth. Broke them on his mother's nipples. Once tried to breathe, and broke all his ribs. Even had a tail. Lost that with his first excrement . . .

That's disgusting, said his wife.

. . . Yes, but not to forget, first conceived without being asked. A couple of cells . . . Didn't know what he'd be. Figured the mammal category. But couldn't tell in the dark whether he was going for an aardvark or a flying squirrel. So just continued in fetalness. What else could he do? Knowing, of course, whatever he was to be he already was. That out of the great catalogue of species he was finding his animal without his having to do anything . . .

Oh, the poor bunny, said his wife . . .

from *Willow Springs*

The Rivals

◊ ◊ ◊

Happiness, in the fairy tale, comes hobbling
disguised as a hag. And the prince takes pity
on her, bringing her to bed, not knowing this

is happiness, thinking this is just a hag who
for some moral he values beyond comprehension
has made this trial of his magnanimity,

and no sooner does he embrace her than she
becomes an exquisite young maiden
with no past and no future apart from his.

So a man I thought my enemy came to haunt me,
featureless at first, in the dusk of dreams,
then turning slowly toward the daylight

until at last, in profile, I recognized
my old rival. He will have his revenge,
I thought, sending that face, more hideous

than anything of nature's cruel devising,
to flame up in a wall of sleepless rage
between me and all that I must see to do.

And my God, I thought, this is like love
who taught me her lesson years ago, though
she was beautiful and this is a death's head.

My enemy came to haunt me, tirelessly
until, desperate, I kissed him, kissed him
dead. Then he slept, long and beautifully.

from *The Paris Review*

A Date with Robbe-Grillet

◊ ◊ ◊

What I remember didn't happen.
Birds stuttering.
Torches huddled together.
The cafe empty, with no place to sit.

Birds stuttering.
On our ride in the country
the cafe empty, with no place to sit.
Your hair was like a doll's.

On our ride in the country
it was winter.
Your hair was like a doll's
and when we met it was as children.

It was winter
when it rained
and when we met it was as children.
You, for example, made a lovely girl.

When it rained
the sky turned the color of Pernod.
You, for example, made a lovely girl.
Birds strutted.

The sky turned the color of Pernod.
Within the forest
birds strutted
and we came upon a second forest

within the forest
identical to the first.
And we came upon a second forest
where I was alone

identical to the first
only smaller and without music
where I was alone
where I alone could tell the story.

from *New American Writing*

BW

◇ ◇ ◇

1.

The world, black and white between the wars
Earlier this century, was sad,
So anemic and so insistent
In its sadness, that people, running
Through the streets after each other loved
To seem alive inside that charcoal.
And so they painted make-up colors,
Science and silence, watching screens
With great character actors, heroes
And heroines, whose gestures you could
Taste in the imagination, reddening
Them yourselves, to think of that bright shame
As happily replacing people
With lovers, nifty in their nipples.
They lived in history, in black and white,
In newsprint and in signs, on Broadway,
Where the large rainbows overwhelmed
The witnesses, all two of them, twined,
Turned into each other labially.
The kiss was big—but so was the mouth,
Coned, or canned and spread (a loudspeaker).
Bewildered protestations failed them,
Perspectivism and black humors,
And they retreated to color tv,
Transvaluation of all prisms,
The silent science of private life.

2.

Why bother? The Brat was saying that
To himself, some forty years later,
The Brat himself now just twenty-five.
The colored screen's cold wars, glass witness
Full of hearsay and information
Made him empty since kindergarten,
All television, a dotty glass . . .
He didn't need to care about much.
It's all what it is, he'd sometimes say.
Now that his wife had thrown him out
He couldn't care. She was a nerd.
She made it in the computer scene
And left him for that successful putz.
Better to be alone—to be walking.
Everyone's really single anyway.
Transvaluation of television,
She'd been his wife for four years, colorful,
But empty, and he'd loved her body,
Not her person. But now he was hurt.

3.

The Brat's favorite food is: Bratwurst.
He wears a white suit to the deli,
And he can't stand or negotiate with
Strong waiters: he knows the polite one.
Those people chanting Happy Birthday
Over their corned beef should shut up.
They ought to shut up and go to hell.
He takes a gulp of his boilermaker.
Those stupid, phony, happy singers
Are driving him up the wall tonight.
He thinks about the way his father
Smirked at the wedding because he thought
The bride too young and the ethical

Nonreligious ceremony phony.
Maybe it was, he shouldn't have smirked.
That stupid little arrogant fart.
How did I get a father like that?
Cigar smoke makes him want to smash
Drifting over from the birthday table
But after a while the boilermaker
Starts to work and calms him down at last.
He sips while watching a game on the set,
Forgetting his doting family.

4.

Cover your ears, the siren's passing!
Brat walks uptown to the West End Bar
And Grille, an inquisitorial haunt.
He can talk there with some semi-friends
Till four a.m., not much questioning
The other weather-beaten people,
Or siren-beaten, but listening
To something soft, their lonely chatter.
They are the voice of population.
Sick of overhearing's intensities,
Myrrh is a resin, an ecstasy,
A bitter fragrance or wood-exude
Scratched with fingernails on the tables.
They talk about how they hate their parents—
Forty and thirty and fifty years old
(Pigeon, from *L. pipire*, to chirp)
Like poptops fastened in passing tar,
Bewildered and bitter, black and white,
These barflies, bollweevils of Broadway
Are no longer looking for their homes.
Battered Wife is here, and Wet-the-Bed.

5.

Quail, kestrel, crane, heron, and resin—
Birds of the barrier. It's 4 a.m. The Bar's
TV, a vanishing tattoo, is taps
Of images. Time for you to sleep,
People, go home, and get some shuteye.
Some channels on all night, Brat stays
Up, at home, watching till the dawnlight's
The same light gray as the screen itself.
And then he sleeps, not turning it off.
He'll visit his parents he decides asleep,
While dreaming by the outdated screen
About them. Beer and bar and water.
He'll go home. They may deliver.
One day he'll be able to afford
Color, but for now he's just between
Malbolge and Malbolge, where he wobbles,
A unitarian compromise.

6.

The Brat's parents are sweet old yiddishist
People. I once had a fiction teacher
In college who said to me sadly
"Why do you put them down in this piece?"
(My parents, he meant), "They sound like
Very nice people." With that, I stopped
Writing stories, feeling slight and rotten
For representing them in assignments.
They were the only subjects I knew
That closely at the time, and like a
Nonfiction novelist I'd betrayed
Intimacy to provide some prose.
Brat, incidentally, isn't me.
This isn't autobiography.
He used to be an acquaintance in college.

I saw him once in Riverside Park
Where he told me some of the stuff here,
And all the rest that's here is hearsay
Got from people who also don't know him.

7.

A landslide of gangs and river bells,
Underwear stores, the Brooklyn Navy
Yard across the river—how many—
How much—population; theys. The Lower
East Side, ticklish old people, antsy
Young ones looking even tireder play
Shmattes, tacos, tic-tac-toe, and bocce.
They live on the eleventh storey
His parents "happen to be" Jewish
Like the universe "happens to" exist,
And so is he. So what? What's the point?
A treacherous, iconoclast height
Overlooked by the Williamsburg Bridge
Which overhears them with a constant
Tire drone, vehicular blue noise.
He doesn't know how they sleep through it,
But he's uptown, a solitary
Confinement, a cathode tube, pure brain,
And a cold turkey, turnkeyed to life.
"Larry," they say, "It's good to see you.
It's been a long time since you been here."

8.

The Yiddish books in their apartment
Indecipherably warming them,
("How many tears lie in the letters")
—A sentimental old teaching song—
("And how much strength you will get from them")

For them it's the only living speech.
English is imperially dead:
Put some English on it. Make it. Go.
English is the mixture of all shlock,
A multi-lingual medley rock.
His silent father sculpts and makes some post-
Retirement money doing portraits
That are mimetically accurate
And lifeless but at times in his life
Has done some lesser more beautiful pieces
For instance one of young Brat a kid
In terra cotta a graceful head
A perfect shape with no conception
Exception affection and liking: partial.

9.

The bridge between barbed wire and beware,
Between the thing and the word, is crossed
Only by wild birds, by actions.
So many brides, so many tv dots,
So many bricks, so many bribes,
Birds on wire trying to be wire . . .
The twenty-one-floor project buildings
All dark and red like the sun's old oven
Turned inside out contain so many
Small alleged "people" (but condemned)
That you might think them kilned to scale
Ceramically—but never removed—. They
Cling to their apartments in the air
Inside a warm red that spurns the world.
So when his father gets on his nerves,
Not having listened to the divorce
Story sufficiently, and then said
When they were looking at that old bust
Of Brat "it's a lot better looking
Than you are now," with a cracking laugh,

Brat takes the piece up in a rage and
Throws it out of the eleventh
Storey, the only copy there is,
A piece of terra cotta flying
Out of the terra cotta building,
Landing on no one but the sidewalk
It breaks into a thousand pieces,
His father's best work, the only one
Touched with some of the grace of life.

10.

"Wobbly, you're crazy, you whiffleball.
Nobody breaks the only skuptcher
His dad did of him just to prove
He can't mess with him. That's going too far.
You need a trip to the Weather Bureau
Where I am sure some Weatherman will
Do your forecast and break your pieces,
Reset your mold. Chip it away.
You need some rehabilitation."
I need not tell you how Brat repented
Or how his father got more silent.
Inordinate clash! Variety!
There's a New York poet who tells
Of meeting his mentally ill son
On the street with a wheelbarrow, in which
He had lots of his father's notebooks, twenty
Years of them, and was going towards
The Hudson to dump them. The father,
Depressed and guilty towards his son, let
Him go. So twenty years of thought were lost.
And why not! for a son! Why not
A kingdom! King David might have said—
But didn't. And the loss was not so total.

There were thirty more years of notebooks
Still extant, including the one in
Which this incident is recorded.

11.

"The window is not a wastebasket
For works of genius," is the first thing
His father said with backward rage once
The reality had dawned on him
That all that rosy clay was shattered,
The image of the boy's beginning.
For a while also the last thing said.
Quick acts never bear false witness, they
Blitzkrieg and dissever—they don't lie!
Utopian dictionaries, which
Have only the words the poet likes
Bear false witness to the language.
Walking behind Aeneas Creusa
Was well-behaved and vanished
She, the beautiful wife, she vanished
While the old man the hero carried
Broke wind and bread and wine and news—
Wade back, sad bather! the tide is in
You should have carried off Creusa
And not that warehouse of Roman virtues
Weather bruised baked apple papa
Her waters break, the baby is born
Thirteen hours after—water, not wine.

12.

Kabbala-sound of the police car.
They hardly dare go to the terrace
(This is housing with terraces) to
Look out and down: co-op cops swarm

Around the shards of Brat's boyhood face.
Other people are also watching
Except their neighbor, Mrs. Shapiro
Who could be said now to be peering
Across her balcony toward them.
His parents call her "Die Shapireh,"
"The Shapiro-ess" you might translate,
And though they like her, she's conclusive
In her opinions of right and wrong.
He broke the bust—will she spill the beans?
It seems the sculpture missed by ten feet
An old man who got very frightened.
Die Shapireh continues to glare.
Hues are mixed colors—high school poem
Word ("the hues of autumn"). Hue and cry.
"What're youse hues doin' in my back
Yard? If you don't get out of here
I'll call the cops. Don' gimme no static.
I been puttin' up wit youse hues too long
And all I want in my playpen is green
And green, nothin' else, and certainly
No uncertain kinds, none o' youse use,
No terra cotta people, no modern
Archaeology of broken lives.
Leee me alone, you understand me?
Don't want no interference no way
Just keep the whole autumn out of this."
Die Shapireh keeps it to herself.

13.

Die Shapireh keeps it to herself.
Her dewlap seems to be soaked in brine
And her eyes gleer with malicious hurt
But she keeps quiet: they'll owe her one—
And no one wants to be a witness
Especially an overhearer

Who didn't exactly see the toss.
The law requires two witnesses.
The sephiroth keep it to themselves.
If you're the only one don't talk.
She heard something—like a bird call—cop
Cars depart, no harm was done. It is
As if a new globe were spinning, and trying
To embrace it with your palms you
Found that the colors were still wet
A mingling dye replays won't heal.
Nothing to do but think of the smears
As an aesthetic that you'd desired.
"I always wanted a blurry globe."
It has a—migratory—beauty.
This simple adequate solution
Wanting the chaos because it's there
Is more intelligent than you'd think.

14.

Nine months later Brat's not much wiser.
Students, to constellate is to stud.
Brat has been horny incessantly
Since breaking that image of himself
And he's found ten girls in these ten weeks
Willing to do the wild lapdance
With him in a couple of hours
After meeting. O.K. Maybe not ten.
(Boundary disputes, the chamberlain's
Domain of judgment in old Poland)
Big women these and bitter young wives
Brat in his life never fucked so much.
In this bar-narrative was some fact.
There were four girls in the ten weeks and
Two of them were actually lively
And warm to be with, if passing through.
Meanwhile his family still sees him:

We of the asm family do not
Get along well with each other
But we meet once a year, if we can—
Enthusiasm, spasm, chasm,
Orgasm, chiliasm, phantasm,—
And have some supper together, praying
All, and for Amen we say "mhm."
It's a new babe and it's a toss-up.

from *Western Humanities Review*

Powers of Congress

◊   ◊   ◊

How the lightstruck trees change sun
to flamepaths: veins, sap, stem, all
on brief loan, set to give all
their spooled, coded heat to stoves called
Resolute: wet steel diecast
by heat themselves. Tree, beast, bug—
the worldclass bit parts in this
world—flit and skid through it; the
powers of congress tax, spend, law
what lives to pure crisp form
then break forms' lock, stock, and hold
on flesh. All night couples pledge
to stay flux, the hit-run stuff
of cracked homes. Men trim their quick
lawns each weekend, trailing power
mowers. Heartslaves, you've seen them: wives
with flexed hair, hitched to bored kids,
twiddling in good living rooms,
their twin beds slept in, changed, made.

from *The Atlantic Monthly*

Voyage

◇ ◇ ◇

From newspapers and clocks and stuffy trains
and banks and yawns and poached eggs and disdain
for any wilderness, I woke to ocean.
For how long did I wait with dumb devotion
for the sounds gulls pour on any harbor?
I don't know. Days, I dreamed of farms where
no water ran, anywhere at all.

It's strange to think how who I was before then
disappeared so fast, and left no more than
my thinning, breasted, monthly-bleeding body,
marked by a certain history but oddly
unfamiliar, like someone whose needs I tended
although the love between us had long ended,
and no companion in my isolation.

At what I thought was night I gave my back
to the prow and pulled across the black
water's surface. The ache of oar on gunnel
and the ripples of the wake gave small rebuttal
to the silence. I stumbled through the dark.
My fingers split. There were no stars to mark
my course, if I can call it that. Mine was

a journey with no destination.
I strained and hoped to catch the chance orations
of any creature who might happen by.

None came. The photocopied waves and I
drank benediction from a murky sun
that swelled and covered everything so one
could not tell sea from sky or night from day.

Longing for a voice (my own, so thin,
terrified me), I made the wind
suffice. Often I had it ask me questions—
who are you?—and imagined its gestures
of attention as I answered: *I am
the tree root's searching tip.* This thought of land
rocked me in its arms until I slept.

Like any castaway I dreamed of earth:
cut-grass breezes, divots of wet turf,
cliff cypresses distorted by coast gales,
all faithful conifers: the keeled cone-scales
of longleaf pines, with prickles at the tips,
larches, firs, whole forests to eclipse
the shallow dish of unremitting ocean.

Sometimes instead of forests I made cities:
narrow streets, cascades of traffic, brittle
heads of garlic heaped in market stalls,
saxophones, cathedral doors; the calls
rising from the dense sidewalk parade
almost drowned the bleak cant of the waves
until I stirred and woke to what was waiting.

Really there were no waves, because no shore
offered itself for them to fall before.
At some point this no longer mattered; in
my need I aimed the vessel's battered chin
into the fists of green waves without number
and did not let the emptiness encumber
my loneliness's efforts at creation.

My only company was the mute presence
of five objects, left by the former tenants
of the vessel, of whom I knew nothing.
These were: a simple broken compass,
whose message—WENS? SEWN? NEWS?—
    I tried for hours
to decode; a sickle with no power
to harvest anything but rust, the haft

worn almost down to steel; a patch of stiff
cloth, once the corner of a sail (all these gifts
had in common utter uselessness);
a book, homemade, handwritten: "Then I let
the children out, then set bread dough to rise—"
and on like that, a journal; and a slice
of mirror, shaped a little like a dolphin.

This last was the most useful of the lot;
with practice I could catch and aim the hot
light lost in the fog and make a beam
that bored into the boat and made it steam,
then smoke. I'm sure if I'd kept at it longer
I could have burned it and myself to cinders.
I don't know why I didn't. For some reason

it was the ragged, dirty bit of sail
that brought me closest to that blank despair
with its agonizing taunt of wholeness
and rescue; and it was the compass
that brought me back. I stretched myself on those
four solid letters, releasing the hope
that the still needle would start to tremble.

Where could it have pointed, anyway?
I saw myself less as a castaway
than as a prisoner, standing trial
by keeping vigil over crawling miles

of empty, infinitely barren sea—
but the watch became the sentence served to me,
and the jury, and onlookers, and the judge.

For some reminder of what past offense
might have earned me such harsh recompense,
I surveyed my body, parched and brown;
it flinched under my watching and let down
the last red husks of that month's refusal
to bear a child, to become she who will
be splayed and split and swollen and betrayed.

Thirst pressed against my closed throat like a brand.
From a great distance I watched my hands
scrabble at the poor skiff's bloodied ribs
to catch the stream and lift it to the lips
I could no longer feel. The steady blood
grew insistently into a flood
that turned my floating cell into a shambles.

Of course I'd killed nothing; but as I stood
barefoot in my own blood, awed, I could
not escape the shamed pride of a butcher:
smeared with death, alive, exultant, sure
beyond words that murder and nourishment
are fierce comrades. My cunt and mouth and breasts
were suddenly not it, nor she, but I.

Soon after that the current's set and flow
started to seem purposeful, although
I didn't search for what that purpose was.
The wind had no voice. How to get across
how swept clean of any hope I felt?
The stamping, shouting crowd my heart had held
lay annihilated, even the ghosts

of my five former unknown companions
disappeared into the silent canyon
of peace inside me. What they left behind
were objects I could see and touch and find
a daily, present use for. These crude tools,
the sturdy boat, the gray sea, and my new
hollow calm and I arrived together

at a moment I couldn't have foreseen.
Hard rain started, the current picked up speed
and I saw my sky was not a sky at all,
horizon to horizon, but a wall
of living flesh, and my sea the river
of a body. Every gusting shiver
brought more light. Ahead the true sky opened.

This wilderness of beings, each alive,
the mismatched stars, humped moon, the flying
fish, the slippery, leaping population
of porpoises, the jokes and lamentations
of whale song humming in the hull finished
my confinement. Now there is the solace
of food, sickled thrashing from the ocean,

familiar cadences of light and dark,
the changing shades and textures of the water,
dear as a face. I've started to remember
faces, and to use the shard of mirror
to find my own, with something like affection.
Stranded like anyone, the isolation
made solitude, I try to understand.

from *Grand Street*

In Violet

◊ ◊ ◊

In the deepest folds, conceived
stroke by stroke to clothe the Virgin,
blue pigment blushes, empurpled
by brushed advances on a body
that wavers like any other
under the dogmatic drapery—
blushes and matches the moistened edge
of her unkissed lips. Somewhere
back of even thicker shadow,
a robed husband recedes—an angel
gets on with it, mouthing,
like the lily blaring from his hand,
injunctions beggaring belief—

this the shade of first bloom
where it labors through snow
to deliver of a greenish ache
something inviolate, stamping
the yard's much-amended foolscap
with its seal, not holding the night.

from *The Gettysburg Review*

LINDA GREGG

A Dark Thing Inside the Day

◊   ◊   ◊

So many want to be lifted by song and dancing,
and this morning it is easy to understand.
I write in the sound of chirping birds hidden
in the almond trees, the almonds still green
and thriving in the foliage. Up the street,
a man is hammering to make a new house as doves
continue their low cooing forever. Bees humming
and high above that a brilliant clear sky.
The roses are blooming and I smell the sweetness.
Everything desirable is here already in abundance.
And the sea. The dark thing is hardly visible
in the leaves, under the sheen. We sleep easily.
So I bring no sad stories to warn the heart.
All the flowers are adult this year. The good
world gives and the white doves praise all of it.

from *American Poetry Review*

THOM GUNN

Cafeteria in Boston

◊ ◊ ◊

I could digest the white slick watery mash,
The two green peppers stuffed with rice and grease
In Harry's Cafeteria, could digest
Angelfood cake too like a sweetened sawdust.
I sought to extend the body's education,
Forced it to swallow down the blunted dazzle
Sucked from the red formica where I leaned.
Took myself farther, digesting as I went,
Course after course: even the bloated man
In cast-off janitor's overalls, who may
Indeed have strayed through only for the toilets;
But as he left I caught his hang-dog stare
At the abandoned platefuls crusted stiff
Like poisoned slugs that froth into their trails.
I stomached him, him of the flabby stomach,
Though it was getting harder to keep down.
But how about the creature scurrying in
From the crowds wet on the November sidewalk,
His face a black skull with a slaty shine,
Who slipped his body with one fluid motion
Into a seat before a dish on which
Scrapings had built a heterogeneous mound,
And set about transferring them to his mouth,
Stacking them faster there than he could swallow,
To get a start on the bus-boys. My mouth too
Was packed, its tastes confused: what bitter juices
I generated in my stomach as

Revulsion met revulsion. Yet at last
I lighted upon meat more to my taste
When, glancing off into the wide fluorescence,
I saw the register, where the owner sat,
And suddenly realized that he, the cooks,
The servers of the line, the bus-boys, all
Kept their eyes studiously turned away
From the black scavenger. Digestively,
That was the course that kept the others down.

from *The Times Literary Supplement*

History

◊   ◊   ◊

When the knife slipped and cut deeply into the fingerpad
as he whittled a stick or trimmed ham from the bone,
at first he felt nothing, aware only of the nearly insensible
line on the skin. Always he imagined for one heartbeat
that he might undo the error and prevent the upsurge
of consequent blood: Such was the character of Juvenis,
who remembered always the doomed legions marching
as they left the city, their big arms swinging, or daydreamed
that the airplane halted inches from the rockface,
like the photograph of an airplane. In my only vision,

I Senex await calmly the formation rising rounded
from the finger's tip:—brilliant, certain, bountiful.
Now, pacing my battlements among sentries, I observe
how terrorists burn athletes; terrorists dynamite
the former ambassador of the executed prime minister;
terrorists sentence the kidnapped president for crimes
against the children they will never father or mother:
They shoot him through the head and stuff his body
into a Japanese sedan's trunk on a suburban street
where the regime's corrupt engines sniff him out.

In the trench there were several corpses. This was in France.
The heels of one stuck out from the dirt of the trenchwall,
the scalp of another. The most dreadful thing we saw
was an arm in field-gray with a hand, dead-white and wearing
a signet ring, that protruded from the wall of a saphead.

Wherever we dug for our safety, we dug into corpses,
more ours than the French. Whenever a mine exploded,
a chowder of flesh splashed through fog and gunsmoke to mark
our positions. Shreds of a Frenchman hung from the branch
of an apple tree. This was in May. This was in Vauquois.

For four hundred years and sixteen generations, I kept
my castle while vassals baked flatbread.
Hoplites protected the confluence of rivers. When plague
squatted in the streets, or when the brawn of Germany
crossed the river to cut soldiers and horses,
peasants and pigs turned wild in the hills. Drought starved,
flood drowned:—Then shires rose in the valleys again.
Bowmen and arquebusiers left bones in the Low Countries.
Seven generations built the wall. For a hundred years
redheaded barbarians walked through a gap in the wall;—

but Danegeld accumulated for bribes and fortifications.
Cabbages kept over winter. Grapes ripened into wine.
Boys gathered the eggs of birds in the June twilights.
Oaks cut for the cathedral roof left acorns behind
for pigs in the diocesan forest; then oaks grew
three centuries under the care of foresters, father and son,
to replace cathedral beams when the deathwatch beetle
chewed them hollow. And now when my managers fly
to Chicago on Tuesday and divorce in Santo Domingo
on Wednesday and cremate their stepchildren on Thursday

without learning on Friday the names their grandmothers
were born to—they weep, they drink a Manhattan straight up,
they tremble strapped to electrodes on a table.
When he assumed the throne Juvenis concentrated
on cost-effective methods for exterminating barbarians
under the boy's illusion that he might establish
permanent boundaries. When his Reichsmarschall Hanno
concluded the Rhine, Juvenis required him to find
a defensible, durable, allweather overland traderoute
from Cornwall to Cathay: Tin boxes preserved

aromas of Lapsang Souchong. John Ball and Spartacus
assemble plutonium for love, constructing a device
to reverse history's river. Titus Manlius scourged
and beheaded his own son for disobedient heroism.
We carried Bhutto to the gallows on a stretcher.
He weighed eighty-seven pounds, a sufficient weight;
he asked the hangman to expedite the matter.
Our imperial goal is simple and simple our mottoes:
PEACE FOR ETERNITY   NOT LIBERTY BUT ORDER.
Meantime as president-emperor I Senex employ

in the execution of governance the expedients
of postponement and triage:—These are the rules of rule.
What in our youth we considered solutions, what our public
relations officers with flourishing trumpets call
"Triumphs of Diplomacy," or "Our Leader's Military Genius,"
are stavings-off. When we stopped supplies for our camp
besieged on the Blue Nile, we gained petroleum and wheat
for the Manchurian campaign; Masada proved no obstacle,
nor the Wall. We strangled Vercingetorix
to purchase half a year. If a thousand decapitations

provide us a century of grain growing, water progressing
along aqueducts, and cattle freshening each spring,
who will not unbind the fasces and sharpen the axe?
Greek fire burnt Saracens at Byzantium's castle
and swamps over the same ages advanced and receded—
as now in the sour pond a pickerel chokes; as now
a whip-poor-will dies unhatched in her frail shell.
Whenever mobs rise against torturers and murderers,
torturers and murderers rise to take their places
and Blues massacre Greens. Men enslave women

again and chop the beggar's hands off and tie
the homosexual's wrists to the killing post
and execute him with prostitutes and moneylenders.
Our former prime minister is dispatched by a single jurist
who empties a machinegun into his stomach.

Our Leader sends a note to the Arbiter, his obedient
counsellor, who opens his wrist in the bath while speaking
wittily with his entourage. But he dies too fast:
Slaves bandage his wrists. Remembering purpose at dawn,
he removes the gauze. Tiberius beheads six Jew doctors.

By Palmer Canyon the lemons in the irrigated groves
grow smaller each year. Here is the Republic's grave,
boneyard of Erasmus and Hume, Florentine gold
and azure, Donatello's bodily marble, graves of money
and liberty. Vertical barbarians ascend, the child armies
of passive ignorance. I Senex, president-emperor,
peering through cataracts, note that Greek fire has only
for the moment prevented Viking and Turk and Bolshevik
who scale my fortifications with devoted outrage
and howling for plunder break the small-paned windows.

from *The New Yorker*

Kinneret

◇ ◇ ◇

As the dry, red sun set we sat and watched
  Them bring the fish in from the harp-shaped lake.
At night my life, whose every task is botched,
  Dreams of far distant places, by mistake.

They tunnelled through the mountains to connect
  The raging ocean with the inland sea.
Dreaming of you, I wander through some wrecked
  Historic region of antiquity.

We played unknowing for the highest stakes
  All day, then lost when night was "drawing nigh."
The dark pale of surrounding hemlocks makes
  Stabs at transcendence in the evening sky.

Out on the lake at night one understands
  How the far shore's more distant than a star.
The music playing right into my hands,
  I took the measure of my dark guitar.

Beauty? the dolphins leap. But for the truth,
  The filtering balein of the great whale.
Age? it's more gullible than flashing youth:
  The ending swallows the beginning's tale.

Far from the freeway and its hoarse, sick roaring,
    He can still listen to the wildwood's sigh.
Across the world the shattering rain was pouring:
    Tears merely glistened in my childhood's eye.

Out of the depths I call for you: the water
    Drowns it, as if that sound were its own name.
Enisled in height, she learned what had been taught her:
    From closer up, the sky was more of the same.

Her thought was silent, but the darkness rang
    With the strong questions of a headlight's beam.
He walked around the lake: the water sang
    An undersong as if it were a stream.

The wind was working on the laughing waves,
    Washing a shore that was not wholly land.
I give life to dead letters: from their graves
    Come leaping even X and ampersand.

Below, the dialect of the market-place,
    All dark *o*'s, narrowed *i*'s and widened *e*'s.
Above, through a low gate, this silent space:
    The whitened tomb of wise Maimonides.

Only a *y*, stupidly questioning,
    Separates what is yours from what is ours.
Only mute aspiration now can sing
    Our few brief moments into endless hours.

The merest puddle by the lowest hill
    Answers the flashing sunlight none the less.
I harp on the two flowing themes of still
    Water and jagged disconnectedness.

I lay in a long field; eleven sheep
   Leapt from a barge onto the grass, and fed.
She cleared the wall and leapt into my sleep,
   Riding her piebald mare of night and dread.

Dressed like their foes, nomadic and unkempt,
   The emperor's legion crept across the stream.
Only as her great rival could she attempt
   The soft parapets of her lover's dream.

The voice of the Commander rang in us;
   Our hearts in stony ranks echoed his shout.
The cold, bare hills have no cause to discuss
   What the thunder among them is about.

Musing at sundown, I recall the long
   Voyages across shoreless seas of sand.
Shuddering at dawn, I call out for your song,
   O isle of water in the broad main of land.

What speck of dust fell on my page of strife
   And mixed its coughing with the prose of breath?
The pensive comma, hanging on to life?
   The full stop that sentences us to death.

From his blue tomb the young sun rises and
   The marble whitecaps pass like dancing stones.
A boy, somewhere in an old, arid land,
   Sat carving spoons out of his father's bones.

Windward, the sun; a galley on our lee
   Rolls gently homeward; now its sail is gone.
This miracle the moonlight once gave me:
   The sky lay still; the broad water walked on.

What cannot be seen in us as we stare
    At the same stretch of ordinary bay?
Her constant dreaming of the Immermeer,
    My half-lost moment on the Harfensee.

In bright, chaste sunlight only forms are seen:
    Off-color language gives the world its hue.
Only in English does the grass grow green;
    In ancient Greece the dogs were almost blue.

The bitten-into fig does, without doubt,
    Show forth that blushing part of which we've heard.
Resemblance turns our language inside-out:
    Pudenda is a self-descriptive word.

He fought Sloth in her arbitrary den,
    And grew bored long before he could defeat her.
I stop—something is too pedestrian
    About the iambs in this kind of meter.

Footsore, his argument gave out and slept
    In the unmeasured vale of meditation.
In marked but quiet waves the water kept
    Time with the heartbeats of an old elation.

This night in which all pages are the same
    Black: the Hegelians must shut up shop.
It seemed when, smiling, you called out my name
    The humor of the noon would never stop.

He parsed his schoolboy Greek, the future more
    Vivid, where rich, strange verbs display emotion.
My glass of dark wine drained, from the dim shore
    I scan the surface of a sparse, gray ocean.

They built beside a chilly mountain lake
   The prison of particularity.
The sun is blind now; only the stars awake
   To see the whole world mirrored in the sea.

The sea's a mere mirror wherein you see
   Something of the gray face of the high sky.
Far from shore, the dark lake relays to me
   The lie of the old, silent land nearby.

The everlastingness of childhood's summer
   Evenings itself skyrockets and is gone.
As if great age would evermore become her
   The far-lit winter night reigns on and on.

Snows on the far, long mountain in the north,
   Seen from the lake, are never reflected there.
Gazing at distance, I keep setting forth
   Unwittingly into the thoughtless air.

We stand our ungiving ground, our unpaid mission
   To creep through fields or scamper across the town.
Still at last, supine, we learn what position
   Earth took on the great issues of up and down.

A kingfisher flashed by them on their lee
   To lead their thoughts toward a blue yet once more.
My tears blur world and water and I see
   Each seed of flickering lake, each drop of shore.

The dry, unsinging river that runs south:
   Somewhere along it we must some day cross.
The memory of music in my mouth
   Sticks to my silence now like leaves, like moss.

Some husbandman will plow where now I row;
  My lively wake will be the long dead road.
Drowning our songs, the river will flood and go
  Mad, as if flowing were itself a goad.

My mind's eye, wearied of distrust, soon turned
  To surfaces, of which it then grew fond.
She meditated on the mud that churned
  Up from the fruitful bottom of the pond.

Down in undreaming deeps the heavy carp
  Fed, while above the shining surface trembled.
Was it my voice that spoke for the bright harp?
  Or was it a heart the singing lake resembled?

Some say I mutter; some, that I reconditely
  Shout: but meanings, like words, like air, expand.
Some fragments hurt you when you grasp them tightly,
  Some feel as if they were part of your hand.

Every dog has his day, and the worm turns
  Nasty within the hard, absorbing grave.
The heat of August threatens as it burns
  Our hearts with the dead cold of winter's cave.

The wind turned to the hard hills and wondered
  At their cold heads and then began to hum.
My white and faulty mortar should not have sundered
  Under the grinding of this cardamom.

Pale cliffs descend below the sea and steep
  In the full silence, calm and unconfounded.
He broke through the thrumming surface of his sleep
  As if some lake-shaped instrument had sounded.

from *Harp Lake*

Twenty-five

◇ ◇ ◇

from *The Novel*

A white bear slides beneath the ice.
It first appeared in *Tristram Shandy*, Chapter XLIII:
"A white bear! Very well. Have I ever seen one?
Might I ever have seen one? Am I ever to see one?
Ought I ever to have seen one? Or can I ever see one?"
Reading of one, you have one.
The white body of words isn't a woman or man.
It's a shape that carries them both,
Shaking like meat, insolvent as water.
The author has stood at a thick glass panel,
watching a polar bear swim underwater,
its long legs gracefully striding.
The author has ridden a cow from Happy Valley
to Stormy Brook, the cow of patience and real events.
The author would mount a turtle, the turtle of elegance.
A black swan would appear to the writer,
beating its significant wings.
The sky was blue as a penguin's eye.
Talk of fever and teething.
People dead in another country
and Martians sending postcards home.
It was a time of resolution with no ending,
insistence with no beginning.
There was urgency and style, variation's blinking light,
and everything imagined piled in a seething heap.

Aides-Mémoire made sand blow into a shape.
The sound of a sentence came into the room,
gave a pathetic wave, and quietly went out of existence.
It was almost a song, nearly a speech after dinner,
alas on loan, amassed a fortune, amo, amas, amat.

To project my being there,
I sang a little song,
its furious blot of a heart
wrinkled like a plot.
They quickly gave the answer
to which I was the question.
They had prepared a "nor"
for the "never" we'd extended.
Ping Pong in the neighboring room
and Ping Chong on the phone.
Salesman asleep in sister's bed.
Striking yourself underwater
in a chilly little novel
yet to be written in Poland or France.
First kiss in Ocean Grove, naked lady
in the house next door. Killing the cat
with a .22 rifle. Norman Workman drowning.
Photo looking out of the album.
The abortion is now in Wisconsin.
The name of the town is Malta.
Just a quick note to let you know
I value the comments you made
at the symposium. Indeed, I will buy you lunch
and further discuss the matter.
If the man I'd killed was Father,
who was this in my bed?
The bomb struck out in all directions,
passing through Swanee and Dave
on the way to the light beyond.
Lieutenant Gorge looked into the hole
that used to be their camp.
Only a pair of shoes remained,

filled with fucking blood.
Poetry is important fiction,
thought the dead Marine.
An empty swimming pool
filled with the fucking neighbors.
Bob's dog's picture's great.
The flat didn't wave; it groaned,
tossing and retrieving its shadow.
Everything was the color of mud,
even the blood in his eye.
The only writer in any language
less exciting than Proust.
Robert Musil's philosophical music
turning to metal jelly.
Rising from the trench,
Gorge could see the sky.
When the second bullet came,
his body bucked and started,
then rocked back on its heels.
Lieutenant Gorge lay flat in mud,
against whose mothering
nothing stirred, a semblance
remembering buoyant water.
Things shaken in a hat.
Looking for stars up someone's sleeve.
The relative unimportance
of oppositional gestures,
regardless of the sonnet.
In the moribund ward,
masters of tastelessness
perform a Chinese firedrill.
The tacky sleeze of the soul's decor
could not be underscored.
We must take action against this sea of woes.
We must close the virulent houses
where torpid images writhe like water.
My mother is buried in Indiana,
low on a sloping hill.

My grandmother lies high in the dark,
by a river in Virginia.
The shadowy evidence photography provides.
Lost in the grain of being.

from *New American Writing*

The Good Reason
for Our Forgetting

◇ ◇ ◇

Who would have the day back you saw coming in dreams
long before the actual stood like a flower

gone bad in the jar? The dreamed drunken driving,
steering from the back seat, or the garden of mazes

and he forever turning as you felt your way along
the broken bushes. Even the street of barking dogs

you finally walked through, empty-handed, pointed
to one thing. Who would have it back?

After the fact, you throw the stinking water out,
scrub the sink and turn into the new life

as if dreaming, knowing it is no dream, knowing
better. Although, some nights, you smelled it,

didn't you? A certain dissembling deep in his eyes
you could never reach, not with love

not with fearfulness. You smelled, you were almost
sure of it, something like flowers,

the beast too long neglected. But that was before,
and long before you heard the story of the boy

and his father, how left alone for three days
they played cowboys, and how the father fell

on the first day, fell down and stayed there, playing
dead, the boy thought, and how he tried

to lift his father's head, tried to feed him
to make him stop, feed him breakfast, and how

he didn't stop, not for one minute, not once.
Who would have the day back when it happened to him?

Or the day before the day when he imagined himself
a boy, and deservedly happy?

Like the night, when the light from your lamp fell
on your face with what seemed an affectionate look.

from *Partisan Review*

Heat Lightning in a Time of Drought

◊ ◊ ◊

I lie awake, not by choice, and listen
to the crickets' high electric trill,
urgent with lust. It pulses on the humid night—
and even the breeze would be sweltering
if there were one. Heat lightning flashes.

The crickets will not, will not stop.
I wish that I could shut the window, pull
the curtain, sleep. But it's too hot.
Just hours ago my neighbor, drunk, stood outside
and screamed, *Want some! Want some!* He bellowed it

as cops tossed him against their car, cuffed him,
threw him in the back seat—*Want some!*—and drove away.
He screamed so clear, so loud, I was afraid
I'd somehow made him up so he could scream
what I knew better than to say out loud

although it's August-hot and every move
bathes me in sweat, and we are careless,
careless, careless, everyone of us,
and when my neighbor screams out in his yard
like one dog howling for another

I call the cops and turn him in,
then lie awake in my own sweat, remembering
the friend who, at a party on a night this hot,
walked up to me and propped her chin on my chest.
She was slightly drunk, the love-light

unshielded in her eyes. We fell in love,
lived together for almost a year,
and, one day at supper, the light fixture fell,
exploded on the table. As we sat stunned
glass flew around us in a long, slow-motion blossoming.

But we were unhurt till I reached
to brush it from her face, and then four drops of blood,
no more, ran down her cheek, rose-red. On TV
I'd seen a teacher dip
a long-stemmed rose in liquid nitrogen.

When he withdraws the rose, it smokes: it's frozen solid.
He snaps one petal, frail as isinglass,
and then, against the table, shatters it.
The whole rose blows apart, as we did,
my friend and I, though not perhaps so violently.

And then one day the doorbell rang, and when
I opened the door a salesman said, "Watch this!"
He stripped my bed and vacuumed it.
The nozzle sucked up two full cups of flakes.
"That," he said, "is human skin." And as I stood

beside the bed, refusing to purchase,
staring at her flesh and mine mingled
inside the measuring cup, I thought,
"She's gone two years, she's married, pregnant, and all this time
her flesh has been in bed with me." Don't laugh.

Don't laugh. That's what the Little Moron says
when he comes home early from his work
and finds his wife in bed with another man.
Enraged, he fumbles in the dresser for a gun.
The other man leaps through the window,

shattering it, and the Little Moron puts
the gun to his own head and pulls the hammer back.
His wife, in bed, the damp sheets pulled up to her breasts,
starts laughing. *Don't laugh!* he screams.
Don't laugh—you're next! It is the wisest joke I know

because the heart's a violent muscle, opening
and closing. Who knows what it might do:
by night, the craziness of dreams; by day,
the craziness of logic. Listen!
My brother told me of a man wheeled, screaming,

into the hospital, a coke bottle rammed
up his ass. I was awed: there is no telling what
we'll do in our fierce drive to come together. The heart
keeps opening and closing—swelling, clenching—like East Ohio,
where fire still burns, a century underground,

following the rich black veins of coal, rearing up,
occasionally, to take a barn, a house, a pasture.
And though I wish that it would rain tonight,
I think of that long, unquenchable fire,
so hot and constant, unlike the heat lightning

that, three months into a summer drought,
blinks on the hot horizon as if it promised rain.
It can't. But I, like many other people in these parts,
have stood out on my lawn, my head thrown back,
and watched it hungrily—all dazzle, all light—

as once, awakened by my parents' shouts,
I tiptoed down the cold linoleum
and looked around the kitchen door.
We need two hundred bucks! my mother yelled,
and swept the table clear of all the pennies,

nickels, and dimes I'd counted into dollar piles.
Two hundred bucks? my father shouted back.
He kicked the fallen coins against the fridge,
and Mother reached back and punched his jaw.
They shared slow, looping blows, took turns until,

exhausted, they fell across each other's shoulders,
tented there, beside the kitchen table, teetering.
Air hissed. The hot night stank of scorching flesh.
The hiss grew louder, trilled and spat,
as thin smoke curled up from their bodies.

Blue flames, like twin blowtorches, shot
out of their backs, and suddenly soft fire
enveloped them, and underneath the fire they swayed,
slow dancing, as they merged to long long flame,
then dwindled to an airy pile

of ashes, fine and white as baby powder.
Handful by handful, I choked it down.
And then, before I went to bed that night,
I found and ate each scattered penny, nickel, dime.
I gagged and wept. But still I ate them all.

from *The Georgia Review*

Every Day There Are New Memos

◊   ◊   ◊

Fact-fluffed, appended with dates, they drift down, O bountiful
  accountings, O grim disbursements!
I take them from the box. I take them from the groggy hand
  that moved for no more purpose
Than to record the slow minutes of meetings where nothing
  was really resolved,
But I keep thinking that those names hoisted above small towns
  and splashed
With orange paint across the silver tanks of water towers
Mark the final defeat of the block plant and soybean fields,
  and I keep believing
That those luminous nicknames, Blade and Superstar, as they
  surface in Queens or the South Bronx—
Spraypainted so artfully on the sides of subway cars that one
Has to look two or three times beneath curiosity and admiration
  to make out the lettering—
Represent our surest victories over glass, concrete, and steel.

In a time of vague and courteous doubt, in the quantum amnesia,
  in the fretful face
Of failed loves, I have put my faith in the locally signed work:
  John Payne
Hardware, Red Mullins Rebuilt and Guaranteed Transmissions,
  Bob and Stump Stevenson

Of Stevenson Brothers Furniture. Everywhere else the family
    business is lost. Everywhere else
The anonymous acme of the great purchase regards and subsumes
    all minor concerns,
Subcontracting for its own name a tone: soporific, indigenous
    to no tongue,
But projecting a gray aura of confidence, of accurate machines.
This is why I work very hard to make out the name Delray Brooks
    under the Prudential sign.
I imagine him sneaking out at night in his old shoes to repossess
    his city with paint,
Writing soliloquies on sidewalks, aphorisms in public restrooms—

But we do not truly read them, the entries are so profligate
    they seem cracks
Ramifying up walls, flawing the marble patina of our days.
Yet in just this dubious way, the leopard and the fox express
    their clear boundaries,
The braggart signals to the saint from across the abyss.
Whatever was brought low is lifted high. Whatever was
    nameless shines.
The insides of buses are like phone books listing the fierce
    and the promiscuous,
And in the woods, the lovers who carve their initials deep
Into the beeches are like Whitman reviewing his own poetry.
    Proud flesh,
Proud glamor of the self, my joy now is to sign this openly,
    I who often wanted to be no one
And dreaded more than stitches the roll approaching my name.

from *The Georgia Review*

An Awful Lot Was Happening

◊   ◊   ◊

When you come down to particulars everything's more complicated.
Fervent gestures in the South U restaurant, even the Greeks
behind the counter listen. Burned draft cards,
lamb's blood poured over files at the downtown Draft Board
—acts of resistance, moral values begun.

Saint Augustine in *De Trinitate* didn't see memory structured
by public events. A great moment in my life—not purple clouds
which excited my longings in Nichols Arboretum;
instead, the rumor cancer spread through Lyndon Johnson's brain.
Saint Augustine in his *Enchiridion ad Laurentium* didn't see

her dress and bra across the only chair in my small room
at One Thousand Four Olivia. I couldn't comprehend
whether more words might mean more, my greed, untrained,
not yet certain of its justifications.
And there was war. And from the bluff above the Huron River

rain of starlight above Ann Arbor's lights, three, four
bell chimes ringing in the Tower. It wasn't Rome.
She dizzied me with excessive desires and thoughts.
What I wanted from all my talk of beauty, she said, was power,
and because of it, she said, I'd cause much suffering.

Although I never bragged misery—maybe once. I was serious.
What was I supposed to do when I heard you could be beaten or
　　　　worse

in the neighborhood in Detroit between Linwood and Dexter,
the color of your eyes wrong. These are facts.
Professor Fuller's response that no one taught them to be quiet.

Glass from the bank's large plated windows all over the street.
I telephoned—line busy; tried again a few minutes later
—no answer. Where is she?—the verge of tears.
Swinburnian dactyls merely went through my ears. Advocated
concision, spatial range, temporal disposition of simple language.

And didn't the spokesman for the Black Action Movement
also receive a number over three hundred in the draft lottery
and attend graduate school?—I came back.
Three years later, every space turned inside out.
January, noon, beams of light across you shake out. Confused,

whirling joy when you slid off me. I leaned
again to embrace you. Uniform Commercial Code on the table.
On the dresser a cup of coffee, tulips in a vase.
How to explain to myself how much I love you.
In the Law Quadrangle—my peer. He commanded Marines

in the Anhoa Basin. What did I know—what hookworms are like.
What it's like to shoot a Viet Cong, popped from a hole, in the eye.
A piece of metal in your kidney. It's too easy
to be sheep, he concludes, softly. Or too difficult,
I conclude, softly. He stares at me and whispers something.

I answered I intended to maintain freedom; my brother railed.
What, or who, collides in you beside whose body I sleep?
No work at Tool & Die, Motors, Transmission, or Tractor
while the price of American crude rises another dollar.
There really wasn't enough work anywhere. And there was war

God the spirit of holy tongues couldn't release me from,
or from my dumbness. Pressured—delirious—
from too much inductive thinking, I waited for
the image in whose presence the heart opens,
and lived to sleep well; of necessity assessed earth's profits

in green and red May twilight. —You came toward me
in your black skirt, white blouse rolled at the sleeves.
Anticipation of your eyes and your loose hair!
My elementary needs—to cohere, to control.
An awful lot was happening and I wanted more.

from *Poetry*

DONALD JUSTICE

Dance Lessons of the Thirties

◊   ◊   ◊

Wafts of old incense mixed with Cuban coffee
Hung on the air; a fan turned; it was summer.
And (of the buried life) some last aroma
Still clung to the tumbled cushions of the sofa.

At lesson time, pushed back, it used to be
The thing we managed always just to miss
With our last-second dips and twirls—all this
While the Victrola wound down gradually.

And this was their exile, those brave ladies who taught us
So much of art, and stepped off to their doom
Demonstrating the foxtrot with their daughters
Endlessly around a sad and makeshift ballroom—

O little lost Bohemias of the suburbs!

from *The New Criterion*

Getting Dressed in the Dark

◇ ◇ ◇

June, yet the roses are still asleep in their black dormitory,
Illusions of grandeur dissolving mid-air like sugar in weak tea.

Soon, they will hoist themselves out of their despair,
Muscling in on the atmosphere with their fragrant animosity.

The hedge-clipper's bicycle, a pair of spectacles at this distance,
Leans against some reticent shrubs.

For blocks, the lawns are strewn with tattered burlap.
Brown, stained with the sweat of dew, it could be clothing

Tossed from your dreams, the entire wardrobe
Of your dread unconscious pitched out

As your body, the quivering pelt, slept on
Clad only in bracelets of air.

In the bedroom, surrounded by four-legged non-creatures
—Table, chair, dresser, bed—

The body rises, shifting its inner tropic from swamp to tree,
Pats the floor for its shoes, places a thumb

On each side of a sock—the mugging grin of a boy
About to stick out his tongue—

And slowly, as if dipping a foot into cold water,
Rolls the puddle up over each ankle.

Upright now, wrapped in a drape by the window, see the bit of cloth
With flaps like arms that lies chest down on the neighbor's lilacs?

A pale shirt? A smoking victim from that night you thought
You were Deianira in a world without a doting Heracles?

Soon, the red velvet she might have found to enchant him
Without killing him will hang at the top of every ladder of thorns.

from *The New York Review of Books*

Three Songs at the End of Summer

◊   ◊   ◊

A second crop of hay lies cut
and turned. Five gleaming crows
search and peck between the rows.
They make a low, companionable squawk,
and like midwives and undertakers
possess a weird authority.

Crickets leap from the stubble,
parting before me like the Red Sea.
The garden sprawls and spoils.

Across the lake the campers have learned
to water-ski. They have, or they haven't.
Sounds of the instructor's megaphone
suffuse the hazy air. "Relax! Relax!"

Cloud shadows rush over drying hay,
fences, dusty lane, and railroad ravine.
The first yellowing fronds of goldenrod
brighten the margins of the woods.

Schoolbooks, carpools, pleated skirts;
water, silver-still, and a vee of geese.

•

The cicada's monotony breaks
over me. The days are bright
and free, bright and free.

Then why did I cry today
the way babies cry, for
an hour, with my whole body?

.

A white, indifferent morning sky,
and a crow, hectoring from its nest
high in the hemlock, a nest as big
as a laundry basket. . . .
                    In my childhood
I stood under a dripping oak,
while autumnal fog eddied around my feet,
waiting for the school bus
with a dread that took my breath away.

The damp dirt road gave off
this same complex organic scent.

I had my new books—words, numbers
and operations with numbers I did not
comprehend—and crayons unspoiled
by use, in a blue canvas satchel
with red leather straps.

Spruce, inadequate, and alien,
I stood at the side of the road.
It was the only life I had.

from *Poetry*

Six Hamlets

◇ ◇ ◇

SMOKING HAMLET

HAMLET
> To be, or not to be: that is the question.
> Whether 'tis nobler in the mind to suffer
> The slings and arrows of outrageous fortune
> Or to take arms against a sea of troubles
> And by opposing end them.

*(*HAMLET *lights a cigarette, inhales, exhales, and walks offstage.)*

LA COMTESSE DE BERCY HAMLET

(Enter, en toute élégance, Anne, COMTESSE DE BERCY.*)*

COMTESSE
> To be, or not to be: that is the question.
> Whether 'tis nobler in the mind to suffer
> The slings and arrows of outrageous fortune
> Or to take arms against a sea of troubles
> And by opposing end them.

(At the end, a strong wind blows and her clothes swirl all about her.)

Team Hamlet

(Six team members *stand in a line facing the audience. Each says, in order, one syllable of Hamlet's "To be, or not to be" speech. After every six syllables, or after every poetic line, the* team members *change their posture—they sit, kneel, turn sideways, stand backward, lie down, etc.)*

Little Red Riding Hamlet

*(*little red riding hood's *house; outside it, a forest; then* grand- mother's *house. While an offstage* voice *recites Hamlet's speech, the story of Little Red Riding Hood is acted out in dumb show.)*

VOICE
  To be, or not to be: that is the question.

*(*little red riding hood's mother *gives her a basket.* little red riding hood *leaves home.)*

VOICE
  Whether 'tis nobler in the mind to suffer

*(*little red riding hood *encounters the* wolf.*)*

VOICE
  The slings and arrows of outrageous fortune

*(*little red riding hood *walks on to* grandmother's *house, goes in and finds the* wolf *in bed disguised as* grandmother, *and questions him.)*

VOICE
  Or to take arms against a sea of troubles

(The wolf *attacks* little red riding hood. *She cries out. The* woods- man *arrives.)*

And by opposing end them.

(The WOODSMAN *kills the* WOLF, *splits him open, rescues* GRAND-MOTHER, *and all is well.)*

HAMLET REBUS

(A very big, white EGG *is onstage.)*

HAMLET
To be, or not to be: that is the question.

*(*CHICKEN *comes out of* EGG. HAMLET *smiles, and continues.)*

Whether 'tis nobler in the mind to suffer

(Enraged FORTUNE *figure comes on and attacks* HAMLET *and the* CHICKEN *with slung stones and arrows.)*

The slings and arrows of outrageous fortune

(After slinging and shooting at HAMLET, FORTUNE *disappears.)*

Or to take arms against a sea of troubles

(Big noise of waves, tempest, crashing, screams and moans. HAMLET *draws his sword.)*

And by opposing end them.

(He rushes off. The sounds cease.)

Transposed Hamlet

(HAMLET, *wearing avant-garde clothes.*)

HAMLET
    Tube heat, or nog tube heat: data's congestion.
    Ladder tricks snow blur Hindu mine dew sulphur
    Tea slinks end harrows have ow! Cages portion
    Orc tube rake harms hay canst a Z oeuf bubbles
    Ant ply cop posy kingdom.

(*He goes crazy.*)

from *One Thousand Avant-Garde Plays*

The Ransom

◇ ◇ ◇

Without knowing
How or why, I was standing in a square,
Meeting with a high-placed officer

Who said I'd been selected as the go-between
To bring a ransom set upon the head
Of one I didn't know and never would.

I took the job and promised to deliver
The sack of cash; then slept in a fever,
And woke immersed in duty and the hour

The thing I had to do would be fulfilled.
People assembled at the chosen spot;
I approached them, ready to play my part,

When a voice in the gathering called out,
"They've changed the producer!" The producer?
The words, null and void, were loud and clear.

"But this is life," I said, clinging to sense:
"No one produces it. It's not a show."
They didn't understand my point of view.

In medias res (as if a god had died),
A world dissolved and roles were reassigned
For reasons that remain unspecified.

So there I stood while someone else went on:
No practiced understudy or rising star,
Just the result of a shift in power;

A change that came to pass not for anything
I'd done—no fatal flaw in character,
Sickness of soul, was the root of the matter—

Only a minor detour in the plot,
That a producer new to the scene
Had cut the part played by the go-between.

What could I do but swallow my pride
And walk away (I wasn't paranoid)
After handing back the bag of loot,

Another worthless prop, for all I knew.
Birds were singing, buds flaring in the blue,
So why should I mourn? But what of the life

Of one unknown—without a face or name—
Whose strangeness was becoming what I am.
Better to turn to the natural world,

Following a twist in nature's plot, than live
Where youth is a decoy and time a ruse
Sowing the grass with rue. Before I choose

To drink the bitter draught of history,
I'll hail the tragic muse; then drain the glass,
And put out all the lights and watch the news.

from *Grand Street*

104

Dog Poem

◇ ◇ ◇

Fierce and stupid all dogs are
and some worse. I learned this
early by walking to school
unarmed and unprepared
for big city life, which they
had been bred to for centuries.
The chow who barred my way
snarling through his black lips
taught me I was tiny and helpless
and that if he grew more determined
I could neither talk nor fight,
and my school books, my starred exams,
my hand-woven woolen mittens, a gift
of my grandmother, would fall
to the puddled sidewalk and
at best my cold sack of lunch
might buy me a few moments
to prepare my soul before I slept.
I inched by him, smelling the breath
hot and sour as old clothes.
He did nothing but rave, rising
toward me on his hind legs
and choking against the collar
which miraculously held. Later,
years later, delivering mail
on bicycle in the new California,
I was set on by a four-footed moron

who tore at my trousers even
as I drummed small rocks off
his head. I dreamed that head
became soup, and the small eyes stared
out into the bright dining room
of the world's great dog lovers,
and they ate and wept by turns
while I pedaled through the quiet streets
bringing bad news and good to
the dogless citizenry of Palo Alto.
The shepherd dog without sheep
who guards the gates to sleep wakens
each night as my tiny boat
begins to drift out on the waters
of silence. He bays and bays
until the lights come on, and I
sit up sweating and alarmed, alone
in the bed I came to call home.
Now I am weary of fighting and carry
at all times small hard wafers
of dried essence of cat to purchase
a safe way among the fanged masters
of the avenues. If I must come back
to this world let me do so as the lion
of legend, but striped like an alley cat.
Let me saunter back the exact way
I came turning each corner to face
the barking hosts of earth until they
scurry for cover or try pathetically
to climb the very trees that earlier
they peed upon and shamed. Let their pads
slide upon the glassy trunks,
weight them down with exercise books,
sacks of post cards, junk mail, ads,
dirty magazines, give them three kids
in the public schools, hemorrhoids,
a tiny fading hope to rise above
the power of unleashed, famished animals

and postmasters, give them two big feet
and shoes that don't fit, and dull work
five days a week. Give them my life.

from *The Gettysburg Review*

Teste Moanial

◊ ◊ ◊

Actually: it's the balls I look for, always.
Men in the street, offices, cars, restaurants,
it's the nuts I imagine—
firm, soft, in hairy sacks
the way they are
down there rigged between the thighs,
the funny way they are.
One in front, a little in front of the other,
slightly higher. The way they slip
between your fingers, the way they
slip around in their soft sack.
The way they swing when he walks,
hang down when he bends
over. You see them sometimes bright pink
out of a pair of shorts
when he sits wide and unaware,
the hair sparse and wiry
like that on a poland china pig.
You can see the skin right through—speckled,
with wrinkles like a prune, but loose,
slipping over those kernals
rocking the smooth, small huevos.

So delicate, the cock becomes a diversion,
a masthead overlarge, its flag distracting
from beautiful pebbles beneath.

from *Exquisite Corpse*

Condo Auction

◇ ◇ ◇

I

The salesmen, disguised as befuddled policemen, waveringly
surrounded the art collector.
They had driven capably all the way from The Hague to
East Harlem.
The owners shrewdly viewed their plight with this distorting
but comforting disposition:
Turned upside down, whatever its form, the picture acquired
greater reality.
Although fully responsible, they waived membership in the
drought administration: "Not our kind of time."

We have world enough, and time, and comfy, reliable
appetites.
If you're looking for lucidity, forget it—our script is
polysynthetic, womb-like, versed.
We vector into frumpy solitudes and start doodling there.
From time to time we buy dinner for handlebar impresarios,
then have to tell them to get lost.
You cannot view our plan as a concept, but it's more forgivable
as a plan than as a glossary.

II

I swung desperately on the announcement tree, favoring one
hot hand then the other.
You came into my view as a dead-mute twentieth-century

painter, with a few gross cachou "Bombay spheres"
  in your hair.
I said I had been a visionary nocturnal lad, avid for
  opportunities of longing and learning.
I begged you, you forgave me. Your period was as late as
  a rusty weathercock.
I became a glass man wistfully purveying culture cans.

III

Va-t-il nous déchirer . . . ? Under his wildly wrenched wing
  foaming above the pebbles
He permitted me to keep score. Because it was so déjà vu,
  foreign, and funny,
He looked like Akhenaton. Because this raised the question,
  were those guys all previewed for one showing?,
He gave me the space to establish my female dreams. Smug
  as he was,
He was an Indian giver and made me return (by messenger)
  his yucca-green skin-diving flippers.

He became a cultural virtuoso. Adrift, not knowing where
  to apply,
He unwound the lost beat of Albigensian song. By means of
  inapplicable vocal calisthenics,
He decided what happened in the Danish play. Out of
  revocable fourteenth-century glosses,
He vamped the original Pythagorean dialogue. Imbued with
  the aura of Greece,
He summoned me back, holding my arm under his as evening
  fell on Persepolis.
He unfumblingly drew the parallel: a material one.
  Comparing every tradition with another,
He was absorbed by a finer if no less gripping melancholy.
  A voluble kind of pilgrim,
He pampered my godless wastes. With what he feebly called
  in-voicing,

He attained a stasis between mortality and immortality.
  Unfeelingly, peacefully,
He authored vanity comic books about his hero—a pastoral,
  glacial hero in an age of automobiles.

Where are they, the inevitable ones, the bearers of
  hermaphroditic grace?
They had passed out of the slums and suburbs uncowed by
  purpose and residual feelings. Neither fleeing
Nor seeking, contented by the bread of coincidence, they
  are to be found on the move not there but everyplace.
They are not seen specifically to have moved. They live,
  but we love them,
Who appear to us wearing formidable shoes and our own
  vintage clothes.

IV

Voyez, voyez, j'ai les mains pleines des fleurs!
She forced my imagination, because she had become a law to
  be discovered
Punctually. She had all the gravid charm of a brand-new
  Trojan horse.
She vouchsafed my wobbliness as though one was an
  appealingly masculine exile.
Next came the offer to purvey a model of her black-and-
  yellow wing machinery.

V

They were forever told that the old bastard was compulsively
  giving it away.
They refused to recognize something obvious (obvious like
  the living bejeezis in his pew):
The reviewed poet's transparent tongue comfortingly stapled

To his lapel. They soared in marvelous twilight definitions,
    their bodies rinsed and dried. They
Had a longing for actual things, such as party favors, or
    a blast of motors, a whiff of scallions, swallows of
    salt and virgin oil.

VI

I gave you a painting by Di Pisis, and you matter-of-factly
    strung it up on your bedroom wall. To me,
The "Glass Man" was the portrayal of an honorary banner that
    half reveals a sarcophagus under a recumbent marble male.
You saw in it a princely curtain half concealing a prone
    man turned white with the beginnings of violent pleasure.
I could not perceive if I was to focus my gaze on the foreground
    cloth or on what lay beyond it.
I keep veering through gropy wishes and dreams: you refuse
    me entrance to your tomb.

My valid hand stretched out to you. You blew your nose in
    a handkerchief printed with statements from the *I Ching*.
You put your fingers to your mouth before proving you were
    a true blonde.
Even if my foremost concern was to get answers, the sharpness
    of your gaze instructed,
"Patience." Then you turned into the hedged lane of beeches,
    its unfallen leaves an intense crepuscular yellow.
After your example, I took off my clothes, sure that you
    saw me, that you would give me back what you saw.

VII

He refused to be anything but a guide. Knowledgeable, alert,
    unprevaricating,
He suggested that the search for verbal results to some puzzles
    would lead to setbacks. Dogmatically,

He left me with whatever strength I had. Seeing in me
   qualities that busily escaped me,
He wore dyed-leather suits, left his red hair mussed, and
   gave his benediction to the most casual passing traveler.

VIII

We see that the luscious green girl who works at the dime
   store is privately gathering rubies.
We can tell that she blurs some other object—a fiddler's
   fiddle, which plainly remains as visible as she.
Our craft is drowned in morning glue, the bevy of our souls
   drips oil.
We have been yanked away to a puny commerce of clocks and
   graves.
We become devoted to abstraction—abstraction that
   transforms people into red, yellow, and green.

IX

We are called the favorably settled poets, a category best
   restricted to men.
We are now turned into an object of antagonism, a specific
   antagonism channeled through the chilly space
Of the present. It's no problem for us if drummers and
   guitarists decline from one verity
To the next: they will only convulse themselves in a green
   frenzy, beyond our pale.
At their probable return, we can vouch that we engender
   antagonisms of our own.

Ton souvenir en moi luit comme un ostensoir!
She walked in front of the enshrined host, publicly scattering
  pyracantha berries and dog violets.
The cortege proceeded, with its dull gold highlights, its
  smoke, its boy voices (such harsh thirds!),
With her. The event was distantly heart-rending in its
  squandered faith, which became her past first years.
She left the charming realm of a visibility just seen, of
  a wound just felt.

Le ciel n'est pas plus pur que le fond de mon coeur!
What was hard was telling if, in all that numbed activity,
  the reference was
Herself. Her bloodless face, mauve eyes, and white-blond
  hair flashed through the interstices
Of cottonwoods. She had no desire to travel, to begin again,
  nor did she expect the Yukon to come to her.
She kept bees and walked—unnetted, tidy—among a vocal
  mist of bees.

My inclination was to seek out new possibilities of craving,
  of comprehension,
And I found my body tight in your livid arms, and a black
  bay (down) and a black sky (up).
I believed you and would trust you because you primly recalled
  cavernous blue light.
As you moved away, later, last of all, you said, "Don't bother
  to catch up on your sleep."
At sunup a boat dropped me in a grove of yews, on a stiff
  but ascendable coast.

XI

The dispossessed string crew, they who forged themselves
  women's veils, bodily pursue
Untitled desire where ruins are perversely camouflaged among
  the disintegrations of history,
Where singers, worrisomely batlike, dart from ground floor
  to roof level.
They live but are not seen to move. We respect them. We
  forget them.
Unshod, the musicians vanish, asking, "Sweet love, how like
  you this?"

XII

The real thing—could she formulate or contrive it, in
  her brown study?
She claimed to have a Buddhist future but watched the clouds
  with anthropomorphic ingenuity.
With me she acted nonchalantly poetic, helping me to get
  past my unappeasable flus and avidities.
In the thick of raw incredulity it occurred to her to give
  up thinking about "animal" and "mineral."
She acknowledged her privilege of being overcome by fierce,
  serious zeals.

We undressed her beautifully, privately, taking our time
  and hers.
From her breasts we cast off two veils, strips of sumptuously
  opposing primary colors.
Unbound from the starry silk folds of a waistband, a civil
  dimpling was shown.
We turned her on her belly to shed the paisley pantaloons
  so dramatically girding her loins.
We concluded that she was in no way the object of our
  impervious intentions.

To us it looks as though humans march through rows of vapid
but juicy casabas.
We intuited divisions glazed over one another casually and
transparently, down to an embedded periwinkle.
At dawn we dipped a toe at the lakeside cove, each body
mindful of its mother's dead father.
We followed a procession of masks—smiles portraying a
sense beyond vulgar glee or sadness.
Vengefully we followed them back to a lake and cursed the
dappled, red-fleshed trout.

XIII

"Oui, puisque je retrouve un ami si fidèle."
More than once she vowed to escape my boggled memory of
her. To run after her produced contrary results.
At times, on olive-shadowed, sea-sucked rocks, I plied
dreamily towards her forgotten absence.
She promised to possibly screw me if I gave up any hope of
nailing her down.
At midnight, in Very shadows of public moonshine, I made
the mistake of understanding her.

XIV

He made his wished-for vaseline link-up: an invisible century.
In a gray fogey's dance
He fagged me in John's carnival hole. When, in boyish
Christian times,
He murdered me, emitting the beep of a wayfaring
mathematics,
He discovered death connecting life and faith. Indirectly,
hypothetically, even bumblingly,
He trained himself for a gentler if no less busily clownlike
vesper melancholy.

So you make the avoidable plunge, stepping gingerly into
    the chill. I knew
Myself to be an untalkative architect from elsewhere, my
    pate speckled with mica.
You considered yourself an avowedly morning person, getting
    business done, unperplexed by past closures
Or by voided goals—hardly my case, who watched you purely
    out of greed, who wanted
What you were about to have. You lapsed into your waitress
    role, facing my table with empty stone goblets.

XV

Within their chamber music they have professionally
    concealed a machine gun.
It is aimed at the weaving tail of the great piebald music
    fish. Lesser schools
Publicly follow lines of a glittering fugue they have chosen
    not to mind not choosing.
Perfervid color-seeping bullets whisk by them in lettuce-green
    light.
The musicians still provide any willing taker with their
    professional pleasures.

from *The Paris Review*

Kidnapped

◊ ◊ ◊

1

Time's not on your side, the doctor says,
Nor the dead who'll rot on a silver plaque,
As you'll see again the men jostle the morning leaves,
And among the graves, in a far field,
The women, too, where the bones weep.

2

Is a chapel in the city opening its doors,
An old monk squatting in the histological dark,
Are the pills on the table, will they bring peace,
A white knife entering the cupboarded flesh
Now the carcass breathes? . . .

3

As we live we'll remember dying in dreams,
Remember the psalm and the grain and the wedding ring,
The believers in the blood and the firstborn,
Remember the thunder that lies awake in the sky,
Or screams in the pillow till we sleep.

At the hospital a nurse has struck another vein
And it's blown up to the size of an egg,
The doctor apportioning the hours to come:
Look, the boats, he says, afloat on a marble shore,
And here the zero chances of immortality . . .

Still, if time's not on your side,
Then beaded with stars every link of the journey
You'll meet a season you'll never get clear,
When the distances are drugged and the scars must deepen,
Though, perhaps, for once, no longer in pain.

We'll yield our names to a dull valley,
Our names hum and burn in the trauma,
The people asking: *why not do it, why delay,*
As fighting the self, the self's ogling a runaway
Child with a copy of "Kidnapped" in his backpack . . .

Where's he off to, that boy, so chaste in the evening,
What adventure is left, and who shall he be,
So driven by himself to forget himself,
The blast of a shotgun rifling the air
And a moon swimming out of a last vision?

from *The New Yorker*

Showing Us the Fields

◊ ◊ ◊

We watched you waving as we pulled away, the ground swept
Bare of you, the rearview mirror holding you
Until we careen around a curve, as stars must into new fields
Forever be moving away from us in all directions.

At the edges of fields evergreens contain all colors necessary
Or imagined, recollected to stay our gazes in the local.
Behind us, a house's lights go on like a dream
Remembered late the next day. We disappear into the border,

As empty as when we arrived and watched you in a mirror
While you straightened your hair in another bare room,
The table already set. You told us your fear then,
That you would run out of words after reaching the edge of a field

Surrounded by evergreens—you wrote it down and it has remained
A shadow, not dropping from sight even after moving to the end
Of a rural route with geese stationed around the pond
Swept clean of the sky, swept of any expectations of collapse.

When we arrived, the cherries were coming into bloom, each flower
Hanging by a slender white thread, as though the trees were draped
In lace, a net of cinquefoil, garlands now said to be the last
Record of the beginning of stars. You showed us the fields:

Sodden, the broken gate, the tracks of wild dogs some say
Have torn apart sheep in nearby fields. You saw them crossing
In to the evergreens at dusk this past winter and wondered
What you would have found if you followed them into that knit

Darkness, at what steaming carcass you would have surprised them,
Or if they would have turned into shadows brushing you with fatigue,
The weight of the sky pressing you into the snow. You stop,
Saying how the words have been coming more slowly each day,

As though each were an excess or a transgression, and emerging
From the evergreens near with the weight of the unspoken.
The evening still bright, we depart and when I say I saw you bearing
An evergreen, what I mean is an emblem of recollection,

Waving at the end of the drive a bough that our car must have
Snapped off, waving as though to sweep the air of the day-
Guillotined dreams, waving us off to our homes after the long drive
Sweeping into sight the first stars, the bough rising, falling.

from *Boulevard*

The Fifties

◊ ◊ ◊

For ten years Boss was always on a trip.
From Chicago or New York he'd phone the house
To say goodnight or check up on his son.
The boy was always shy and studying,
So Mother-Wife would respond with little words
Then hang up lonely. So she spent her nights
Until the Open House in '56.
Boss, as usual, was on a plane
As she pulled into the visitors' parking lot.
She stepped out of her Jaguar like a queen,
Or so it seemed to her son who was watching her
From a window in his Home Room science class.
Her ankle bracelet sparkled in black-top heat;
Her red hair caught the sun and softened it.
Clearing his throat, the science teacher stared
As Mother-Wife strolled in and took his hand.
"I couldn't miss our little Einstein's Day,"
She said. "You must be Mr. . . . ."
                                        "Just call me Bill."
Nervously he showed off their displays,
Pausing at the tar pits diorama
To brag about her son's accomplishment.
Boy had been absorbed by Spectacle—
Joanne Stocking adjusting her thick glasses—
The better to see the cow's eye she was slicing.
"Coffee?" said the teacher to Mother-Wife.
She liked his graying temples and blue eyes,

The perspiration veil above his lip.
"The faculty lounge is down the hall," he said,
And turning guided her back out the door.

After that the boy spent many nights
With sitters while his mother stayed out late.
"I've got a meeting tonight," she would explain,
Then take long hours bathing and getting dressed.
Boy could hear her singing through the wall,
And sometimes he would lie down on her bed.
Boss, so busy moving, was far away
And Mother-Wife was singing just for him.

BOY.
I like it when I'm in my room preparing.
Mother works all day. When she gets out
She laughs a lot. Some mornings when it's dark
I sneak into bed with her. I touch her face.
I get this feeling. I touch her and I hurt.

MOTHER-WIFE.
The boy hides in his room, says he's preparing.
He locks the door and I must shake the knob
And yell *Go Out And Play!* I get all weepy,
Never what I want. Tonight I'll wear
A sweater, a tight one, because I am big-busted.
My date will want to lay his head on it,
And if we drive up north and the stars are bright . . .

A horn sounds off outside on the gravel drive.
She glances up then looks again at the mirror.
Her make-up could be better. She pats her hair.
She stands. She pulls her sweater down and goes,
Thinking of the teacher in the car,
Thinking of his head upon her sweater.

Boy unlocks his door and watches her.
Rushing now she pecks him on the forehead,
Smiles, pushes past him, thinking *Damn Him*,
Meaning everyone. The screen door slams.

    BOY.
    After she goes I lock my door again.
    I open notes and pull out all my books
    On polar exploration. I study charts,
    Memorize dates, names, events. I do this
    To prepare for when I'm big, important,
    Maybe President. Or I may leave.
    Outside the galaxy it must be cold,
    And that's where knowing Admiral Scott comes in.

  Boss slams his office door and works the phone,
Loosens the knot of his tie and says hello.

"I got your name and number from a pal
Who says you used to be a cop up north.
He says you're good at finding what gets lost.
I'm on the road a lot, and so's my wife.
You follow me? That's right. No matter what.
I'll come in after lunch if that's ok."

At one a cab drops Boss at Mission Street.
Standing on the curb, he pulls a paper
From his vest and studies the address.
He wads the paper up and throws it down
Beside a leaflet hawking Stevenson,
Then crosses traffic, making drivers stop.
Across the street he bulls into an office,
Charges up a flight of varnished stairs
And bangs upon the frosted glass of a door.
A voice inside shouts
                Open! Come on in!

Inside a woman looks up from her desk
And says *Sit Down*. Boss wrinkles in a chair.
The woman, who is writing, drops her pen.

"Ok," she says. "Suppose you fill me in."

Fidgeting with his hands, sweating a lot,
For the next half-hour the man just comes apart.
He talks about Career, his working wife,
The terrible condition of public schools.
He talks about close calls he's had on planes,
Temptations he's turned down at swank hotels.
Detective lets him talk, studies him,
And now and then makes notes on a pocket pad:

> *Mother-Wife. 26. Clothes design/62 Pacific Ave. One kid/8.
> Guy on road/gal on town. Out when he calls/nervous when
> questioned/moody/headaches every night. Description: 5'
> 8"/115/red hair (long) green eyes/snappy dresser (of course).
> Photo in hand. Tail & Shoot.*

Puffing hard Boss finishes at last.
"Are you a drinking man?" Detective asks.
Boss looks as if he's drained a wet, wet bar.
Red splotches make a pattern across his face
And down the sides of his neck. He rubs his eyes
And in the voice of a little boy says

                                        Please.

"Let's eat up in the hills tonight," Bill says.
"You know. That spot my mother talked about.
Romantic. We'll be inspired by the view."
Mother, long dead, would laugh to see him dining
With a married girl, but he was up
Last night, hungering for sympathy.

Mother-Wife can make it stop, his feeling
That every room just wants to spit him out.
But she has troubles, too, office woes
That butt against and blunt his own distress.

"Two models got the clap and quit today;
Our Paris shipment met an airport bomb.
I'm losing eastern buyers and gaining weight."

Together they drink and bitch and feel alone.
The waiter smokes and frowns, forgetting his tip,
And airs his grievance to the kitchen help.
"Why," he asks, "when the lucky ones stop and eat,
Do they pick each other apart and whimper so?"

   Detective finishes her wine and smiles,
Daubing the edges of her street-smart mouth
With a linen napkin. The waiter breaks away
To fill her coffee cup. She tells him no.
He takes the bill out of his vest and waits
Because she makes a show of paying fast,
Her money already crossing the table-for-one.
"Keep the change," she says,

                         and wriggles out,
Hurrying through the piano bar for the door
Adjacent to the parking lot. Outside
She stops, unslings her camera, and shoots.
The couple in focus kiss beside a car,
A tender shot, then climb inside and go.
Detective finds her car and follows them,
Heading east into the purple hills.
The moon is full tonight. She is working,
Shooting rolls and rolls of evidence.
After one the rocking car she watches
Calms itself. The lovers' heads appear.
With cab-light on, Mother-Wife adjusts
The rearview mirror and works her lipstick hand.

At work the morning after a card arrives
For Mother-Wife. She skims it and sits down hard.
Detective steps to her side, places a hand
Upon her shoulder and leaves it.
                              "Let's talk," she says.
The office where they face each other closes
In on Mother-Wife, who sees her love life
Closing down. Detective holds a packet
In her hand. She says
                              "You know what's here."
The only sound that Mother-Wife can make
Is *why?*
                              "Because he paid," Detective says.
"I'll tell him but I'll say the film's no good.
Your husband's moving. I'll give him credit for that,
But he'll get nowhere that I would care to go."
Detective hands the packet to Mother-Wife,
Whose stricken face is a wash of love and hate.

   Zoning out, Bill stares down past his knees
On which he balances his students' themes.
The grading and the writing of remarks
Is long on a Sunday night. His loafers are scuffed,
Symbolic of the way he feels each day
Before ill-mannered classes. His former wife
Once said he'd never leave his science room.
Pre-Mother-Wife he thought she might be right,
But all his options changed the day she took
Her coffee black and stared through him in the lounge.
He'd violated the Scientist's Code that day,
Working with substances he couldn't grasp.
He knew it, too, but turned away from years
Of operating as he'd learned to do.

He rubs the stubble on his face and smiles,
Stares across the room into blue TV.
The sound is off, allowing him to read
Or think as he pleases.

"Touch the phone," he says

He does, thinking of Mother-Wife, of dinner
Last night, parking and rocking in the hills.
A scene from a gangster movie pulls him back.
His left hand falls from the silent black receiver.
The papers slip from his lap to the stained carpet.
He feels heroic in a jaundiced light
And only faintly hears the gravel crunched
By tires on the street outside. He rises slowly,
Trapped by the image, moving toward the window
Where he parts the curtains, staring still.

Reluctantly he moves out of TV,
Turning his head to look out over the lawn.
Two Hammer Men in suits are crossing it,
Resembling men he's watching in the film.
He shakes his head, trying to shake the link
Between his life and what is happening
On TV. The Hammer Men have reached the door.
Their pounding brings Bill fully back to this:

Open it, he thinks, and take what comes.

He does. The Hammer Men are on him fast,
Working on his body like machines.
Bill sees his body used, a specimen,
Curiously broken without pain.
He sees his class, his distant former wife,
The peeled cow's eye upon the dissecting table.
When they break his legs he hears his one loud cry

Despite the rag he gags on. Then Mother-Wife,
The gently rocking car, insistent, yes,
Her nipples, riding high, growing hard,
His life all over hers, like church, then numb.

    Boy suffers in his bedroom, pulling on
His trousers as he listens through the wall.
His father, talking low, sounds like a storm
Through which some random, painful words are clear.
How long? And *why?* The building thunder says.
Mother-Wife is silent, and Boy imagines
Her just staring through her make-up mirror.
Sing! her son commands. To make it right.
But he is willing her to sing in vain.
Alone, frightened, Boy opens his own mouth
And sings, off key, a favorite lullabye.
The morning light is gray. The room is cold.
Thunder builds on the far side of the wall.
Then Mother-Wife runs in and hugs him hard,
Rocking back and forth on the edge of the bed.
Father fills the doorway. Reaching down
He pries the two apart and lifts him up.
Father's face is cruel and pitiful.
Boy wants to kiss and slap it all at once.
Walking into the hall with Boy in his arms
He says
            "Forget about your school today.
I have a surprise for you." At kitchen table
Boy and Boss sit down to spell it out.
Staring down Boss caps the sugar bowl
And wrestles with the grief he cannot pin.
"Your mother's ill," he says. "She's going away."

"How long?" Boy asks.

                        "Until she's right again.

A month. A couple of weeks. It won't be long."

"I want to go with her," Boy says. Boss acts
As if he doesn't hear, but shakes his head
Like some slow, final pendulum. Boy cries.

"There, there," Boss says. "I saved the best till last.
You know the school I went to as a Boy?
You're starting there tomorrow. Happy now?"
Boy blubbers, wiping his sleeve across his nose,
And says
            "I'll have to wear a uniform."

"I'll pick it up today. A blazer and slacks.
You'll look just like I do when I go to work.
Now cheer up, huh? The Jesuits are good!"

    So Mother-Wife departs the galaxy,
Or so Boy thinks, tossing on his bed,
Taking notes from books on Admiral Scott.
He wonders if she'll starve, be forced to kill
A dog and eat it raw. He wants to grow
Up mean and fast, out-run his loneliness
And bring his mother home. The North is far.

Southeast, somewhere, Mother-Wife pulls off
The two-lane highway toward a small motel.
The room is smaller than a limousine.
She feels the change, lights a cigarette,
And sits down on the bed to count her money.
The counting is not long, she notices,
Which means a job hunt sooner than she'd like.
She misses Boy, wonders about Bill,
And even in an odd way misses Boss.
She hesitates, then reaches for the phone.
Boss says hello. He listens. He hangs up.
The caller cries, decides to take a shower,
And gets some sleep with a nudge from seconal.

For more than a year the pattern repeats itself
As Mother-Wife crisscrosses the bleak Southwest.
Sometimes she deals Blackjack in Las Vegas,
Pushes drinks in Bisbee, types in Austin.
Every night her calls to Boss break down.
In Bisbee she is fired for drinking too much.
Her money thin, her prospects all played out,
She calls up Boss and begs to come back home.
Hearing liquor in her voice he smiles,
Relishing the break he's been waiting for.

"First you'll have to fix yourself," Boss says.
Boss states his terms. Mother-Wife agrees.

    Entered in a sanitarium,
Mother-Wife, aided by hypnosis,
Relives the early years of life with Boss:

      MOTHER-WIFE.
      I sipped my coffee in the breakfast room
      And stared at wild roses winding high
      Above the house, tangled in a tree.
      Boss said *I'll cut them if you want me to.*
      I thought of Boss stockpiling, improving us
      By bringing what was free inside. At first
      He only watched the hummingbirds, then hung
      Up cages, hoping they'd like to feed in-doors.
      When flowers bloomed I'd hear his scissors working
      Nervously, as if I'd caught him talking
      To himself about a secret past.

    The session ends. Mother-Wife comes back
To sedatives, a wheelchair ride to bed.
The next day, sitting listless in the sun,
She manages to write some lines to Boy:

Sometimes I wake up laughing I am so happy.
Sometimes I feel the sun. Then I am humble,
A little sad. And I am with you, Love.

from *The Hudson Review*

WESLEY McNAIR

The Abandonment

◇ ◇ ◇

Climbing on top of him and breathing
into his mouth this way she could be showing her
desire except that when she draws back
from him to make her little cries
she is turning to her young son just
coming into the room to find his father my brother
on the bed with his eyes closed and the slightest
smile on his lips as if when they
both beat on his chest as they do now
he will come back from the dream he is enjoying
so much he cannot hear her calling his name
louder and louder and the son saying get up
get up discovering both of them discovering
for the first time that all along
he has lived in this body this thing
with shut lids dangling its arms
that have nothing to do with him and everything
they can ever know the wife listening weeping
at his chest and the mute son who will never
forget how she takes the face into her hands now
as if there were nothing in the world
but the face and breathes oh
breathes into the mouth which does not breathe back.

from *The Atlantic Monthly*

JAMES MERRILL

A Room at the Heart of Things

◇ ◇ ◇

Two rooms, rather, one flight up, half seen
Through the gilt palm-fronds of rue Messaline.

Sparse furnishings: work table, lamp, two chairs,
Double bed, water closet, fourteen stairs;

Six windows, breathing spaces in the plot,
Between its couplings, to enjoy or not.

A poster—Carnival's white eyeless faces.
The ceiling fan. The floor the actor paces

From room to room, getting by heart the lines
Of boards washed ruddier as day declines,

Of fate upon the palm slapped to his brow,
Of verse the instant they are written (*now*)—

His shadow anyman's, chalk walls a trite
Clown-camouflage all comers penetrate.

★

The role he studies—a Young Man in love—
Calls upon self and the eclipse thereof

By second nature. Evenings, dazed from sun,
Earth buries her worn faces one by one

Deeper in fleecy quilts, dusk atmospheres,
Then high-up quivering Hesperus appears.

Just so, the actor, deep in middle age,
Assumes a youth till now unknown. On stage

Within a stanza to be somehow first
Turned inside out and only then rehearsed,

It's this one's pen he seizes, and lamplit
Page he corrects. Soon he may read from it

Tonight's draft of the curtain line (Act II):
"Light of my life, I've made a play for you!"

ᴧ

Reduce, said Malraux, to the minimum
In every man the actor. Brave bonhomme,

Coming from him—! Beret and cigarette,
The worldwide field-reporter style was set

By how he posed, key witness to his time,
Questions of moment, face a paradigm.

We plain folk who believed what we were told
Had seen our crops burnt and our wives grown old

In one same night. Malraux alone took note,
As all who could read, would. Neat, was it not?

Life gave the palm—much the way God once did—
For "living biographically" amid

Famines, uprisings, blood baths, hand to heart,
Saved by a weakness for performance art.

★

Those ivory towers were bric-a-brac. One flight
Of wooden steps, one slapdash coat of white,

Sets the room hovering like a UFO
At treetop level. Spellbound by the glow,

Moth hallucinates and cat outstares
The glamor of dimensions never theirs.

Its tenant treads a measure, lights a joint,
Drawing perspective to the vanishing point

Inside his head. Here vows endure beyond
Earshot of lovers who dissolved their bond;

Whitewash keeps faith with tenements of dew
Already atomized to midnight blue;

And Gravity's mask floats—at Phase XV
Oblivion-bright—above the stolen scene.

★

Actor and lover contemplate the act
So-called of darkness: touch that wrestles tact,

Bedsprings whose babble drowns the hearing, sight
That lids itself, gone underground. Torchlight

Gliding down narrow, redly glimmering veins,
Cell by cell the celebrant attains

A chamber where arcane translucences
Of god-as-mortal bring him to his knees.

Words, words. Yet these and others (to be "tarred"
And "set alight" crosswise by "Nero's guard")

Choreograph the passage from complex
Clairvoyance to some ultimate blind x,

Raw luster, rendering its human guise.
The lover shuts, the actor lifts his eyes.

★

By twos at moonset, palm trees, up from seeds
Big as a child's heart, whisper their asides—

Glittery, fanlike, alternating, slow
Pointers in the art of how to grow!

They have not relished being strewn before
Earth-shaking figures, Christ or Emperor.

Profoundly unideological
Wells of live shadow, they are no less tall

Pillars of strength when—every twenty-six
Millennia, say—their namesake the Phoenix

Comes home to die. (Stylite and columnist
Foretell the early kindling of that nest

—Whence this rustle, this expectant stir?)
The actor robed as priest or birdcatcher

★

Steps forth. The room at heart is small, he smiles,
But to the point. Innumerable aisles

Converge upon its theater-in-the-round's
Revolving choirs and footlit stamping grounds.

Only far out, where the circumference
Grazes the void, does act approach nonsense

And sense itself—seats cramped, sightlines askew—
Matter not a speck. Out there the *You*

And *I*, diffracted by the moiré grid
Have yet to meet (or waffled when they did!),

But here, made room for, bare hypothesis
—Through swordplay or soliloquy or kiss

Emitting speed-of-light particulars—
Proves itself in the bright way of stars.

from *The Inner Room*

THYLIAS MOSS

The Warmth of Hot Chocolate

◊ ◊ ◊

Somebody told me I didn't exist even though he was
looking dead at me. He said since I defied logic,
I wasn't real for reality is one of logic's definitions.
He said I was a contradiction of terms, that one side
of me cancelled out the other side leaving nothing.
His shaking knees were like polite maracas in the small
clicking they made. His moustache seemed a misplaced
smile. My compliments did not deter him from insisting
he conversed with an empty space since there was no
such thing as an angel who doesn't believe in God.
I showed him where my wings had been recently trimmed.
Everybody thinks they grow out of the back, some people
even assume shoulder blades are all that man has left
of past glory, but my wings actually grow from my scalp,
a heavy hair that stiffens for flight by the release
of chemical secretions activated whenever I jump off a
bridge. Many angels are discovered when people trying
to commit suicide ride and tame the air. I was just
such an accident. We're simply a different species,
not intrinsically holy, just intrinsically airborne.
Demons have practical reasons for not flying; it's too
hot in their homebase to endure all the hair; besides,
the heat makes the chemicals boil away so demons plummet
when they jump and keep falling. Their homebase isn't
solid. Demons fall perpetually, deeper and deeper into
evil until they reach a level where even to ascend is
to fall.

I think God covets my wings. He forgot to create some
for himself when he was forging himself out of pure thoughts
rambling through the universe on the backs of neutrons.
Pure thoughts were the original cowboys. I suggested
to God that he jump off a bridge to activate the wings
he was sure to have, you never forget yourself when you
divvy up the booty, but he didn't have enough faith that
his fall wouldn't be endless. I suggested that he did
in fact create wings for himself but had forgotten; his
first godly act had been performed a long time ago, afterall.
I don't believe in him; he's just a comfortable
acquaintance, a close associate with whom I can
be myself. To believe in him would place him in
the center of the universe when he's more secure
in the fringes, the farthest corner so that he
doesn't have to look over his shoulder to nab the
backstabbers who want promotions but are tired of
waiting for him to die and set in motion the natural
evolution. God doesn't want to evolve. Has been
against evolution from its creation. He doesn't
figure many possibilities are open to him. I think
he's wise to bide his time although he pales in the
moonlight to just a glow, just the warmth of hot
chocolate spreading through the body like a subcu-
taneous halo. But to trust him implicitly would
be a mistake for he then would not have to maintain
his worthiness to be God. Even the thinnest
flyweight modicum of doubt gives God the necessity
to prove he's worthy of the implicit trust I can
never give because I protect him from corruption,
from the complacence that rises within him sometimes,
a shadowy ever-descending brother.

from *Epoch*

141

The Wellspring

◇ ◇ ◇

It is the deep spring of my life, this love for men,
I don't know if it is a sickness or a gift.
To reach around both sides of a man,
one palm to one buttock,
the other palm to the other, the way we are split,
to grasp that band of muscle like a handle on the
male haunch, and drive the stiff
giant nerve down my throat till it
stoppers the hole of the stomach that is always hungry,
then I feel complete. And the little
hard-hats of their nipples, the male breast
so hard, there are no chambers in it, it is
lifting-muscle. Ah, to be lifted
onto a man, set tight as a lock-slot down
onto a bolt, you are looking into each
other's eyes as if the matter of the iris were the
membranes deep in the body dissolving now—
it is all I want, to meet men
fully, as a twin, unborn, half-gelled,
frontal in the dark, nothing between us but our
bodies, naked, and when those melt
nothing between us—as if I want to die with them.
To be the glass of oily gold my
father lifted to his mouth. Ah, I am in him,
I slide all the way down to the beginning, the
curved chamber of the balls. I see my
brothers and sisters swimming by the silver

millions, I say to them Stay here—for the
children of this father it is the better life;
but they cannot hear me. Blind, deaf,
armless, brainless, they plunge forward,
driven, desperate to enter the other, to
die in her and wake. For a moment,
after we wake, sometimes we are without desire—
five, ten, twenty seconds of
pure calm, as if each one of us is whole.

from *American Poetry Review*

MARY OLIVER

Some Questions You Might Ask

◇ ◇ ◇

Is the soul solid, like iron?
Or is it tender and breakable, like
the wings of a moth in the beak of the owl?
Who has it, and who doesn't?
I keep looking around me.
The face of the moose is as sad
as the face of Jesus.
The swan opens her white wings slowly.
In the fall, the black bear carries leaves into the darkness.
One question leads to another.
Does it have a shape? Like an iceberg?
Like the eye of a hummingbird?
Does it have one lung, like the snake and the scallop?
Why should I have it, and not the anteater
who loves her children?
Why should I have it, and not the camel?
Come to think of it, what about the maple trees?
What about the blue iris?
What about all the little stones, sitting alone in the moonlight?
What about roses, and lemons, and their shining leaves?
What about the grass?

from *Harvard Magazine*

The Bridge of Sighs

◊   ◊   ◊

If you'll believe me when I tell you I have tried
To understand pleasure, the beginning of pleasure,
You'll know exactly how I watched my mother

That morning lounging in the red plush chair
In the gray, submerging shadows of the parlor
As she talked on the phone: that I stared

With each of my five years at the tender
Curve of her ankle as it moved down the high instep
Of her dry, clean, pale, and perfect foot and over

The toes, underneath to the arch. Oh, it just leapt!
It was the highest, most splendid arch,
More magnificent than the Arc de Triomphe in the newsreels

As the German soldiers marched beneath,
More delicate than the arches of the bridges
Of Venice, built by those gentlemen the Doges,

Paved by the feet of centuries of lovers
And saved from destruction by the American soldiers
On probably the same morning

I watched my mother's foot tense and relax,
And when she smiled down her long body at me,
And stroked my hair, and offered me the smooth beauty

Of her foot, and asked me, yes, to *rub it* just a little,
She said, right into the phone to whomever,
"Ahhh," the *ah* of the beginning of pleasure

That demands, even as it gives itself up,
That leaves you always ready to begin,
Always on the lip of things

Like a young harlot standing on the Bridge of Sighs
Waving goodbye to the soldiers of the losing side,
Waving hello to the soldiers of the winning side.

from *The Atlantic Monthly*

Sun

◇   ◇   ◇

Write this. We have burned all their villages

Write this. We have burned all the villages and the people in them

Write this. We have adopted their customs and their manner of
     dress

Write this. A word may be shaped like a bed, a basket of tears or
     an X

In the notebook it says, It is the time of mutations, laughter at
     jokes,
secrets beyond the boundaries of speech

I now turn to my use of suffixes and punctuation, closing Mr.
     Circle
with a single stroke, tearing the canvas from its wall, joined to her,
experiencing the same thoughts at the same moment, inscribing
them on a loquat leaf

Write this. We have begun to have bodies, a now here and a now
gone, a past long ago and one still to come

Let go of me for I have died and am in a novel and was a lyric
     poet,
certainly, who attracted crowds to mountaintops. For a nickel
     I will

appear from this box. For a dollar I will have text with you and answer three questions

First question. We entered the forest, followed its winding paths,
        and
emerged blind

Second question. My townhouse, of the Jugendstil, lies by
Darmstadt

Third question. He knows he will wake from this dream, conducted
in the mother-tongue

Third question. He knows his breathing organs are manipulated by
God, so that he is compelled to scream

Third question. I will converse with no one on those days of the
        week
which end in *y*

Write this. There is pleasure and pain and there are marks and signs.
A word may be shaped like a fig or a pig, an effigy or an egg
                                                                but
there is only time for fasting and desire, device and design, there is
only time to swerve without limbs, organs or face into a
                                                        scientific
silence, pinhole of light

Say this. I was born on an island among the dead. I learned language
on this island but did not speak on this island. I am writing to you
from this island. I am writing to the dancers from this island. The
writers do not dance on this island

Say this. There is a sentence in my mouth, there is a chariot in my
mouth. There is a ladder. There is a lamp whose light fills empty
space and a space which swallows light

A word is beside itself. Here the poem is called What Speaking Means to Say
      though I have no memory of my name

Here the poem is called Theory of the Real, its name is Let's Call
      This,
and its name is called A Wooden Stick. It goes yes-yes, no-no. It
      goes
one and one

I have been writing a book, not in my native language, about violins
and smoke, lines and dots, free to speak and become the things we
speak, pages which sit up, look around and row resolutely toward
the setting sun

Pages torn from their spines and added to the pyre, so that they
      will
resemble thought

Pages which accept no ink

Pages we've never seen—first called Narrow Street, then Half a
Fragment, Plain of Jars or Plain of Reeds, taking each syllable in her
mouth, shifting position and passing it to him

Let me say this. Neak Luong is a blur. It is Tuesday in the hardwood
forest. I am a visitor here, with a notebook

The notebook lists My New Words and Flag above White. It claims
to have no inside
               only characters like A-against-Herself, B, C, L and
N, Sam, Hans Magnus, T. Sphere, all speaking in the dark with their
hands

    G for Gramsci or Goebbels, blue hills, cities, cities with hills,
modern and at the edge of time

                            F for alphabet, Z for A, an H in an
arbor, shadow, silent wreckage, W or M among stars

What last. Lapwing. Tesseract. X perhaps for X. The villages are
known as These Letters—humid, sunless. The writing occurs on
their walls

                                    from *Sun*

Movie

◇   ◇   ◇

History is not a sentence,
but this is. And though history
is a word, what it names
isn't. And though I'm a person
who puts words next to
recognizable scenes where
your entertainment dollar
is hard at work, and I understand
there's only so much anyone
can put up with in any given
sentence, still there can be no
straight lines in this mass
of air representing itself
visually as broken into pieces,
and temporally as a single car ride with
a unified driver, following
the machine's nose. The landscape
is placed sentimentally on either side
to make the view visceral, poplars,
a starry night, crows over a wheat field,
all engraved in an edible
freeze frame called
taste, that worldly shrine
coextensive with its financial backing
where everything is above average
and the weather gets past the cloakroom
only in the form of haircuts.

It's the pure part, the whole thing,
the last word first, once, and forever.
History is a sob story
that should have known better
except that its head is always being
removed and placed—just this
once, the better to
address you with, my dear—here.
About suffering we are therefore
wrong, the neo-masters, as we use
money to display art,
then write off the money
that mounted the display
in the first place, the only place
in the sun that counts,
up to one and then
it stops, its shade
cool & pleasing, its death
always a story told
—to someone who's not dead, of course.
But if the present is either
eternal or false, like
Tycho Brahe's silver nose,
then what about the calendar,
standing there, a self-
contingent fiction, hands
on hips wide for child-bearing, yet
slim as a jockey's, too, in
a display of semantic undecidability
that American-century language can only
suffer through in a silent
automatic display of arbitrary
displacements. Icarus fell
into the sea long ago. His suffering
is over. His father, the general
whose grandson was born deformed
by Agent Orange, says he would
do it over again. His suffering

is displaced onto the only remaining
figure, the peasant ploughing
in the foreground, just above
the bottom of the frame, the
virile threshold where visibility
stops and deniability starts.
So then grammar *is*
one big evangelical conspiratorial
set of embedding procedures
on top of which certain pleasures
crow to their father in heaven
while far below people get
burned, blown away, or compressed
into expostulations of gratitude.
To call this a language
flies in the face of all fictions
wearing the pre-Raphaelite
cloth-of-gold togas
under which, in every case, beats
the same modernist heart, also of gold,
with an improvised mythic
history on its left sleeve
(so uniform is the power of grammar).
But you have to start somewhere.
What we ordinarily say when
an airplane is flying overhead
is that, though we are not
on board, people are, and thus
collectivisms ground the forms
and directions of every event. If
the particular plane is dropping
white phosporus do we then
exercise our option to begin
to initiate the process of
disinvestment from whatever name
is painted on the fuselage?
A bit slow for the power grid
automatic as electronic relay

tinged with the smell of xerox
rising from the certainty that
the sun would never have to set
if you own enough, and the night
in which all communists are
theatrically black
could be rolled back to the other side
of the world where it belongs
because my earnest face, voice,
and illimitable earning power.
The art of governing, using
the obvious to state the monstrous
—but monsters are human, too—
begins by separating the names
of the countries from the people
who live there. The family
is then placed in the sky,
between the transmission towers
and the individual antenna. So that
mother's not dead, she's only
a picture, feeding me pictures
of what it is to be full.
This nothingness, taken off
the truck and wrapped in plastic,
and weighed, labelled, and priced,
has to have come from somewhere, though,
or else I'm an autonomous phenomenon
and in fact, God. But when a spider
the size of a period
tried to garner some flat dead beetle
as big as a grain of rice
the body, that had been hanging
by some thread, fell.
(Sorry to be taking up space
acting out the vacuity of description
in an antiterrorist program
aimed directly at the senses.)
This happened, fated, on July 11,

1987, the past hermetically sealed
from the present by the obsessive
cries of "I was there, I saw
what was given, plus what I took
by right of need," as the calendar,
a Salome of classic proportions
was stripping it seemed like forever,
while out in the alkaline foyer
of the family ranch the H-bomb
stage-whispered, "I want
to start over," wearing a corset
straight out of the Restoration,
such is the interference of time
with thought's straightahead appetite.
The result is a continuous need
to defend what are called
our needs aching for a clean
language because no word
once spoken, launched without
warning through the fence of the teeth,
can be called back without
getting dirty in another's mouth given
the puritan imperative under which
we still live, trusting
in God to back our money up
with that clutch of arrows
in his right claw
and those words, immutable
and humbling, over which
blurring life histories pour,
straining to keep the sense
single and the biography straight,
all the time floating
down page towards the apocalypse
where silent surface crumples
abruptly to noise. No more
cool grey monuments where A =
A, ironically perhaps, but with a thin,

deferred, cafe-like openness
and portable charm. Political
one-time individual animals
of the free world, born free
and paying at all points
to see the movie, it is you
I satirize with my death's head
outnumbering the camera's gaze
by one when the sun shines,
two when the rain falls heavily
on the thick-slated memory-laden
roofs of past centuries by mistake,
regrettable error, inconsolable
recall. Facts still obtrude
smog-stained facades too modular
to serve as faces, too stressed
by the forced yesses of the building trades
to pass for art, behind which
public turns private
for only dollars and hours
a day. The meter never stops.
There are, right now,
if I can use
such a barbarously out of date
formula, at least ninety covert
ops being carried out
(in the passive voice) beneath
the global visibility of what
the meter shows as merely the
fair price. The unconscious
seems highly armed these days
and to whom do I owe this
articulated dread if not to
the structures of defense
resting permanently on their
freshly killed enemy. But to biologize
these conflicts is always a mistake.
The pathos of the dying transformer-

like termite defending its hill on
Channel 9 to music that remembers
the Alamo if not the Aeneid
leads directly to the ice cream
and the hand held spoon as
stylus of the self that would
sprout leaves and wings and rule
the world even in its sleep,
heavy and fully formal.
Not that anybody's anybody's
slave, mind you. Just don't eat
so much ice cream is all.
These days are as fresh and
uninfluenced as a new pack
at a blackjack table in Vegas
so why do I think chance
has blood under its rug
and lives in a white house?
On July 13, 1987, I just happened
to see an osprey carrying a
small fish in its talons.
Which is not a detective story, marching
backwards to the scene of the crime,
the moment of the proper name,
the murder, known, sensed
in process, the undifferentiated place
where subject and object merge,
warm and unborn. The reader
whose mind has been excited
by the even steps of narration
to an ecstatic acceptance of
unworked time, the golden age,
is prudently to sidestep
identification with either the
dead body or the revealed killer.
But when weapons proliferate
in their pure, pro-life
state, a unique ending for every

person, then thrillers become the public
vehicle of choice, terror and glistening
threats of pain shown
as near as the senses.
Afterwards, there's traffic, the
bad marriage whose second honeymoon
is such an endless bomb.
At least the luxurious
falsity of the leaves on
Route 3 is real enough.
My eyes, raised and lowered
in the age of mechanical reproduction,
produce the show that by definition
can never play in the capital,
since it has no acts
and the book is so open
as to be illegible in public.
Then do I think that words
are really neat, that empty
clorox bottles and star wars manifestos
can keep the dew of alien
dogs off my property? But if
they don't speak the language
even in our own backyard
where in a classic coincidence
the Augean stables revolt
with soap-opera-like regularity
though the cleansing procedures
are untelevisable, then why
is Ollie North said to be
so popular? "I used to wipe
his bottom," marvels a quoted
woman, printed in a kindly light
because a user-friendly oligarchy
really wouldn't hurt circulation
when it's underground, with
weather and traffic on top,
shopping. Consumer choice is now

a church, hands lifted upward
to the shelves, striving to work
free of the curse of original
childhood eating habits.
The idea of the green party
sleeps furiously, and because dreams
can only be televised
one at a time, election results
haven't stopped many bulldozers.
But you can't sell a view
without slamming a few heads
into a few facades.
Odd, how easy the news-like
voice comes over and says,
"I am the agenda,
for reasons which must remain
unconscious as cars acting out
the look of a secure self
whose national habits
have been dictated by the ineffable
mouth of a pre-fabricated history."
But neither do I want to press myself
down onto some woodsy center stage,
or feel myself up frugally
beside a terrifyingly cute pond
picking out the loose feathers
to make myself a down pillow.
Threateningly anthropomorphic, I know
what happened next: Cary Grant definitely
walked out of his house, the movie
was in color, a glorious day,
yellow sun pouring in
under the out of focus green leaves.
What did you expect? You don't
have to say everything exactly
when you've lived here for
centuries and can address
generalized experience

while self-encapsulating the ear
as "you." Down the street,
a firecracker went off
inside a garbage can. It was the
Fourth of July, garbage day, and July
14, 1987, all rolled into one
swaggering twinkle, the copyright
of an eye that looked out
over its entire life
with a happy willingness
to be filmed, truly,
anthropomorphically, at home.
Everyone in quotes
knows the plot from here:
Cary Grant was married
to Katharine Hepburn, a woman
who thought Derrida was an idiot
and repulsed his obscure advances
whenever he came on the screen.
But behind Grant's face and its
European-savage-tamed-by-American-
money smile (movies elongate
the eternal sensual present
of all adjectives) lay a nasty mortgage
as big and secret
as the reversed letters in Freud's
middle name. So Grant had to
in fact rent Derrida a room
in his own home, which, however,
Derrida actually owned, and thus
it was Derrida's, not Grant's, bathtub
that Hepburn reposed offcamera in
(don't even *think* of looking there),
talking about removing ticks from dogs
and recipes for making flan.
And it was Derrida, shockingly enough,
whose arm reached in when she
asked for a towel. If Grant tried

to calm her down and talk to Derrida
about leaving, Derrida would merely
suggest that he read them the book
he was working on, which the audience
knew from bitter experience if not birth,
they'd paid five bucks
for a short escape from the taste of it,
the book was really nothing but
the unbreakable mortgage which
would have them out on the street
clothed but cloned, cold and
improperly sexed in the dark.
Brows knit, Grant was forced
to come up with a plan:
he went to work, which
in his case meant buying
a newspaper—the corporation,
not the physical instance—and struggling
against appearances (at this point
the movie loses all touch with
its conventions). At the office
there's a beautiful secretary,
but she's so rightwing she always thinks
she's playing football. Grant is
tempted (he's always tempted,
and yields instantly, that's his charm
but also what got him into
trouble with Derrida).
And soon we see him
crouching down like a quarterback
behind the secretary with his hands
patient and puritanical
under her bottom as she's spread
in a three-point stance. This
is the creepy part, but apparently
for many husbands in shoulderpads
who only stand and wait,
it vibrates a lot of contradictions

at once. Another deeper rationale
is that in this posture
they represent enough desire
for one, shared between two,
subject and object, proving
that in a world of scarcity
where repression is overabundant
the value of internal restraint
becomes incalculable, while
attending to neurological
sensation becomes more and more
an anachronous luxury.
A nation is a person
(and if an utterly clothed
Cary Grant doesn't convince you
of this all by himself, then
walk naked into the socialist
future with your body
the only badge of realism),
and a nation never dies,
except in the past
or by accident, though sometimes
its processes of reproduction
aren't all that pretty.
So she snaps the ball to Grant
who, though he loves his wife,
has to take it, because inside it are
four-color pictures packed
in freeze-dried prose that prove
Derrida's summer home is
in fact a gulag in Nicaragua,
with lines of people waiting
for buses, for sugar, for paper.
That night, when Grant comes home
with the ball under his arm
the smile on his face means the climax
has begun. Derrida, who senses
the storm brewing, takes out

his manuscript and starts to speak.
But now, thanks to Grant's
sexualized, oppressive and glamorous
hard work at the office,
rather than being out in the cold,
Grant and Hepburn rise knowingly
and retire to the bedroom
offcamera, to the accompaniment of
Derrida's droning nuptials.
The movie has scarcely ended
and already I can hear the cries
of "Focus!" The viewers have to face
something the movie doesn't: continuity
after the end. Nicaragua's still
hanging by sensate threads.
And if presidents still have
charisma, it means that the viewers
have been on hold so long
that they've started to, if not
live there, then camp out, sleep
in cars, or under mortgages
inconstant as clouds.
It's like critics opening
three books at once and writing
"vertiginous" somewhere near
the end of the introductory paragraph.
By now, one day after Bastille Day,
young turks under erasure will
always already have sprung up to
the cry of "Gentlemen, start
proclaiming the due date
of the master narrative in
your sepulchral verbs." Meanwhile, inside
the Bastille itself, specially re-erected
for the occasion by his own
hard work, Celine passes by his
phantasm and has it say, "I
am the Jew," which of course

lets him reply, "I am
Celine." In a gap that seems
to have lasted two thousand years
but really only began
around 1848, they stare, frozen
into a horrific equality,
though the royalties,
humiliatingly tiny as they are,
still only flow toward
the one with the proper name.
But while these pathos-ridden
biographical black boxes take
excellently horrifying pictures
of the economic earth mother
with arms folded over
her breasts, fox fur
around her shoulders and
the head dangling down
toward the pit of her stomach
as she crouches in her den
beside the stone age midden
that yawns beneath the urban
job market, such authorial pinholes
are merely the formally
empty sign of the copyrighted
grave of the father.
The trademark sticks up,
disgusting and compelling, and
the record goes round.
The stable author is the hard
needle, and the record is the
moving landscape flying its
nostalgic date like a red
flag towards which the self,
tethered to a dying technology,
flings itself under the semi-
permanent gaze of grammar.
July 16, 1987, the frozen

actuarial laughter vibrates
my pointed nicked head to sound out:
dismantle your nuclear missiles,
bombs, howitzer shells, chemical weapons,
nerve gas, gentlemen, stop
your reactors now, let your loans
float out to sea. And to show
how realistic the present tense can be,
I want to make room in it for
the nightmarish echoes such baby-hard
demands excite: swollen
with the baulked, slipped passage of time
and opportunities for pleasure
that were forced to go to
dancing school on their own
graves, comes the whispered
thunder of It's not polite
to point It's not realistic
to point It's not effective.
Tears are running down
the clown's face in the
painting above the motel TV
but framing will get you nowhere
outside the frame. "I
call it the schizophrenic
theory, Bob, if we can
make the reader believe that
any word can come next . . ."
where any word refers to
the nuclear bombs Nixon wanted
to have Vietnam believe
he was willing to drop on them
if they didn't stop defending
themselves. As Sade wrote, "The strong
individual merely expresses
in action what he has received
from nature: his violence is pure.
It is the defensive vengeance

of the weak that tries
to name us criminals."
Another way of putting this,
although it costs a couple
of hundred thousand and takes
up to four days to shoot,
is "We don't know you,
but we love you,"
as the large hands, cupped,
visible only as perfect focus,
reach down to shelter
the fragile but wise,
ethnic but cute children. Good
poets steal, bad ones
watch TV, tears
smearing their whiteface
as they display the verbal
equivalent of scars and apply
for grants five months late
each time. But I mean that
to mean its opposite
in a common space
beyond the required reading
of anthologized eternities
where capitalized, footnotable
obstructions like Ollie North—was he
the fat one or the thin one?—
will have stopped bunching
sound into such clots
of powerless fantasy.
But it's July 18, 1987, and
75 degrees. Some things
never change. The past, for
instance, or the present,
that codes and throws down
its dictates at the precise
speed at which the organs
can ingest, detoxify, and classify them.

But since these organs only
exist in the present and,
anyway, levels of toxicity
are set by the producers
of the poisons, this news
shouldn't be taken directly
to heart or allowed in
to your tea if you're nursing.
The liver's relation to coffee
can be expressed in an
equation if you're nervous
or a news account if you're
tired and irritable. The Kenyan's
relation to coffee is closer
to home and so is usually kept
at an untouchable distance.
But do we at least agree
that the human body is paradise
and that the United States
of America is not?
Of course, until history stops
clearing its so-called throat
and starts speaking in understandable
sentences, such hypothetical constructs
as the human body have
only a very limited value.
But description has its uses
even when you're glued
to the tube and model airplanes
are invading your liver.
They arrive slowly
and are deafeningly cute
as they encapsulate
the vestigial childhoods of males
from Rotten to Reagan.
It was more important
than anything in his life
could have been up to then:

if he could get the decals on
absolutely straight it would lead
eventually to a career
in broadcasting and the private
satisfaction of looking back
on the tortuous wake
of one's adolescence pointing
inexorably to the bouquet
of microphones before one's solitary
mouth with the tangle of
cords leading away to the
provinces, Des Moines, Birmingham,
that one can finally leave behind.
To get rid of the past
and be triumphantly attached
to the present by insulated
maternal cords which one
has mastered with one's
trademarked voice which is only
speaking for others, really—
no wonder the boy whose decals
are crooked sobs so hard
there's no thought of talking.
He's lost his chance
of never needing to know
what day it is, or what
city he's in. From now on
it's July 19, 1987, and
there continue to be invasions
and you can't blame them
on the date or the
crooked decals. For two
thousand years poets have been
promising that the emperor's
son is going to turn
the calendar back to one
while the readers, when they're
not attending to formal

state readings, sit staring
at the subtext of
their clock radios. People continue
to die miserably from the lack
of news to be found
there, too, doctor,
every day, as the display
changes a nine to a ten.
Examples can be multiplied
to infinity without adding
up to the great governmental
one which regards all
attempts to establish nondependent
systems of numeration as
so many slaps in the face
of personified free time
and the free world,
where freedom is the same
as the presence of the
agents of that unity.
The airplane is empty (a shy,
self-effacing signifier)
and can carry anything,
this is all there is to know
under the freedom of
information act, and more,
really, than it's good for you
to know, under our way
of life (you can say
system, and you can gather
numbers, but it's my newspaper
and I can stay as anecdotal
as I feel like). The rubble
down the street or south
of the border makes
a convenient boundary before which
any story, to be
a story, must come to a stop.

Out of bounds a few
billion people interrogated daily
by the black and green faces
on the money have to wonder where
those unseen small tight visages
are really planning to put them.
Don't mess with fate
or me, the clock radio
broadcasts, all the centuries are
balanced precariously above us
and can come tumbling down
in a few minutes. But any
realism begins and ends
with its appliances.
Wider claims ultimately depend
on the credit of the audience.
Institutions are made
of matter, as the date observes
its static progress. The theatrical
inevitability of that procession,
beefeaters parading in the dusk,
players who've put up
the numbers being inducted
into the hall, is the
pure gold of the visible
truth. The cardboard, corrugated
tin, and concrete under which
people take shelter from the economic
elements are simply the untrue
static of the leaden age
before reception is to be
perfected. No wonder sound
is so unreliable and our bodies
seem so mismatched. One hears
her mother calling, one hears
his father inviting him to dinner
in heaven that very day.
The audience sees a statue

drag the hero to hell
from which only sequels
return night after night.
Grant and Hepburn have not
emerged from that bedroom,
nor will they ever.
That makes
anomalies of us all,
doesn't it?

from *Captive Audience*

ROBERT PINSKY

At Pleasure Bay

◇   ◇   ◇

In the willows along the river at Pleasure Bay
A catbird singing, never the same phrase twice.
Here under the pines a little off the road
In 1927 the Chief of Police
And Mrs. W. killed themselves together,
Sitting in a roadster. Ancient unshaken pilings
And underwater chunks of still-mortared brick
In shapes like bits of puzzle strew the bottom
Where the landing was for Price's Hotel and Theater.
And here's where boats blew two blasts for the keeper
To shunt the iron swing-bridge. He leaned on the gears
Like a skipper in the hut that housed the works
And the bridge moaned and turned on its middle pier
To let them through. In the middle of the summer
Two or three cars might wait for the iron trusswork
Winching aside, with maybe a child to notice
A name on the stern in black-and-gold on white,
Sandpiper, Patsy Ann, Do Not Disturb,
The Idler. If a boat was running whiskey,
The bridge clanged shut behind it as it passed
And opened up again for the Coast Guard cutter
Slowly as a sundial, and always jammed halfway.
The roadbed whole, but opened like a switch,
The river pulling and coursing between the piers.
Never the same phrase twice, the catbird filling
The humid August evening near the inlet
With borrowed music that he melds and changes.

Dragonflies and sandflies, frogs in the rushes, two bodies
Not moving in the open car among the pines,
A sliver of story. The tenor at Price's Hotel,
In clown costume, unfurls the sorrow gathered
In ruffles at his throat and cuffs, high quavers
That hold like splashes of light on the dark water,
The aria's closing phrases, changed and fading.
And after a gap of quiet, cheers and applause
Audible in the houses across the river,
Some in the audience weeping as if they had melted
Inside the music. Never the same. In Berlin
The daughter of an English lord, in love
With Adolf Hitler, whom she has met. She is taking
Possession of the apartment of a couple,
Elderly well-off Jews. They survive the war
To settle here in the Bay, the old lady
Teaches piano, but the whole world swivels
And gapes at their feet as the girl and a high-up Nazi
Examine the furniture, the glass, the pictures,
The elegant story that was theirs and now
Is a part of hers. A few months later the English
Enter the war and she shoots herself in a park,
An addled, upper-class girl, her life that passes
Into the lives of others or into a place.
The taking of lives—the Chief and Mrs. W.
Took theirs to stay together, as local ghosts.
Last flurries of kisses, the revolver's barrel,
Shivers of a story that a child might hear
And half remember, voices in the rushes,
A singing in the willows. From across the river,
Faint quavers of music, the same phrase twice and again,
Ranging and building. Over the high new bridge
The flashing of traffic homeward from the racetrack,
With one boat chugging under the arches, outward
Unnoticed through Pleasure Bay to the open sea.
Here's where the people stood to watch the theater
Burn on the water. All that night the fireboats
Kept playing their spouts of water into the blaze.

In the morning, smoking pilasters and beams.
Black smell of char for weeks, the ruin already
Soaking back into the river. After you die
You hover near the ceiling above your body
And watch the mourners a while. A few days more
You float above the heads of the ones you knew
And watch them through a twilight. As it grows darker
You wander off and find your way to the river
And wade across. On the other side, night air,
Willows, the smell of the river, and a mass
Of sleeping bodies all along the bank,
A kind of singing from among the rushes
Calling you further forward in the dark.
You lie down and embrace one body, the limbs
Heavy with sleep reach eagerly up around you
And you make love until your soul brims up
And burns free out of you and shifts and spills
Down over into that other body, and you
Forget the life you had and begin again
On the same crossing—maybe as a child who passes
Through the same place. But never the same way twice.
Here in the daylight, the catbird in the willows,
The new café, with a terrace and a landing,
Frogs in the cattails where the swing-bridge was—
Here's where you might have slipped across the water
When you were only a presence, at Pleasure Bay.

from *Raritan*

Sappho Comments on an Exhibition of Expressionist Landscapes

◇   ◇   ◇

Then, she says, a penis is needed, female
artists almost always can use one, taking
charge with tools like brushes and palette knives to
   build up their pictures,

the way men do, spraying great skeins of yellow,
cobalt blue and crimson across the canvas,
rage or quiet made at their will, exploding
   measures of failure,

risking planes, dissolving full spaces, Bluemner
hurling turquoise clouds on a purple field as
blackbirds wheel in formation, Hartley sculpting
   skies out of granite,

oil as cloud made palpable, air as breathless
form accreting mass in its own defense while
ends begin and boundaries disappear.
   This is how men die!

Now, she says, O'Keeffe is my point, consigned to
desiccated bones smoother than silk, unblemished
petals, lilies swollen in heat, faint tensions
    vectored through tunnels,

warm vaginas, moisture of vulvas, furtive
stand-ins, meanings plain as your face: a woman
minus penis making art with her body,
    trapped in her body.

from *Sulfur*

The Shoebox

◇   ◇   ◇

I finally broke down and opened the shoebox
which arrived just weeks after my father died.
All winter I had put it out of sight on top

of the bookshelves where I wouldn't be tempted.
The box was not, as I would have expected,
stuffed with photographs, but packets,

wallet-sized, each with a dozen
"snaps," each sequence a kind of story,
and I couldn't have predicted how they would spring out

once I removed the rubber bands
wound tight as bowstrings around the top—
too late now to put them back,

to stop what I had set in motion—
there is no love in them, only
a memorializing will.

A predictable cast, my father's five
older sisters, their several (only three
between them!) issue.

It wasn't that everyone looked demented,
those spinster aunts, those whiz kid cousins,
but that no one looked like they wanted

to be where they were, in that parking lot fronting the beach,
in front of that penny arcade or movie marquee,
clutching that bulging suitcase. . . .

Only one glossy found its way into the box,
the only shot not taken with my father's *Minolta*:
a puppet without strings, no,

a ventriloquist's dummy, all shocked innocence—
me, glassy-eyed, open-mouthed, plenty of space
between my teeth, dangling above

my father, a rotund, baby-faced, leering man,
and his mother, a slack-jawed, toothless old woman,
greedily gazing up at the child as if she were its mother. . . .

The passersby on Times Square look happy
in a miserable sort of way.
In the mid-fifties laissez-faire seems

to extend everywhere except the family.
I plucked the images I didn't like
but when, after a few hours,

I tried to stuff the slender packets back in
and close the box, even with half
of the photographs smoking in the wood stove

they wouldn't smash down, the rubber bands
would not stretch beyond the limit
they had held for a decade,

yet I felt if I was to sleep, to have peace,
the box had to be shut.
The top had to fit snug around the edges.

from *The Paris Review*

Broken Gauges

◇　◇　◇

Some moments
Hold their grace in ways
　　That seem more
Than momentary though the solitary
　　Believe this to be true
More often than it really is
　　Up late & talking
With old friends I haven't
　　Seen in years
I know fewer of those moments
　　Still penetrate
The past　& if those friends
　　As they sometimes do
In all sincerity & confusion ask
　　How I am these days
I simply say: *Think of me as*
　　A truck with broken
Gauges driven a few times
　　To hell-&-back
By a man a lot like me . . .

★

I was nineteen
& it was midnight & two hours
　　Outside of Winnemucca
Nevada when I finally hitched a ride
　　With a drunken cowboy

179

In a '62 Ford pick-up with four spools
    Of steel cable & part
Of a transmission in the back
    He'd weave back
& forth across the road singing
    Along with the radio
I didn't mind at least I was moving
    At least I wasn't
Back there by the side of the highway
    But pretty soon
With the first glimmer of lights
    In the distance I could
See his tongue starting to work
    Inside his mouth & as
The bar sign came clearer I knew
    There was no way
He'd pass it by without a little
    Something for the road
Then he hit the brakes & we slid
    Half-way across the gravel
Lot before we stopped almost exactly
    At the door & once inside
We hunched down at the bar & started
    Talking like old friends
I bought him a shot of whiskey
    To go with his beer
& then another & then one more & then
    Finally his head just fell
Forward onto his crossed arms & sort of
    Died there   well   *Goodnight*
Cowboy   I lifted the keys
    Out of his jacket & winked
At the bartender saying *I'll go out*
    & get him a blanket from
The truck   & outside I stepped casually
    Up into the cab
Found the right key & hit the ignition
    & as the engine turned over

I looked up to see the bartender's face
    Rise up above the limp
Red curtains in the window so I waved
    I knew that cowboy couldn't
Move a muscle   I put my foot down
    On the accelerator
All the way to the floor & with the gravel
    Of the parking lot spraying
Out behind my tires I fish-tailed out
    Onto the empty highway
Wondering how long I had before
    The bartender phoned
The police & then how long after
    But the night was perfect
Cool & black with lots of stars just
    Clattering around up in the sky
I was going fast but
    When I looked down to scan
The beat up metal dashboard I saw
    The needles of every gauge
Lay motionless   absolutely still
    Speedometer   tach   oil pressure
All glowing there like dead clocks
    With single broken arms
Oh Christ   I thought   I've stolen
    A truck with broken gauges
So I pressed my foot down harder
    On the pedal until I must
Have hit just over a 100 as the first
    Little wisps of steam
Started working their fingers out
    Around the edges of the hood
Then with one enormous white belch
    Of astonishment
The radiator finally exploded
    Boiling water flecked
With rust pouring up over the windshield
    I just held my foot to the floor

181

The smell of scorching oil filling
    The truck's cab then
Like rifle shots & arms snapping
    The rods threw & the engine
Began to pay out its metal treasures
    All along the highway
Accompanying itself with a high whine
    Like steel fingernails
Scraping the eternal black of sky
    & I edged the truck
Closer to the roadside as it began
    To slow   a rolling
Kaleidoscope of nuts & bolts
    Then I turned down a dirt farm road
The truck coasting now   & aimed
    Its nose off the road
& out into the desert where at last
    Its wheels settled in a long
Plush bed of sand & I got out just as
    The engine died in its retching
Staccato steel-warping collapse & walked
    A circle around the old truck
Patting each fender & the twisted side mirror
    Goodbye   then I grabbed my rucksack
& set off walking into the desert
    Until I came to the railroad tracks
Where I began following the rails due West
    Far enough from the highway
I hoped that neither police nor vigilantes
    Could find me & with the faint
Chords of dawn striking behind me to the East
    Ahead I could see on the horizon
The first soft sparks that were the lights
    Of awakening Winnemucca

★

Some say twenty years
Is almost forever & some say it's
    Nothing in a man's life
In all the separate individual lives
    We lead in those years
& I know that I believed in
    Every one of those lives
Or almost every one   at least
    I believed every lie I told
I told for some good reason even though
    Friends said I passed my time
The way other men passed water
    But it was my time to spend & live
My time to take back from anybody
    Who tried to waste it
For me   anyone who was left
    To reason out all those things
That don't stand to reason
    The silence on the phone for example
When you answer in the middle of the night
    To find there's no one
No one there   & sure I've spent time
    In dives & shit-holes
But in some nice places too even plush
    Hotels on high mountain lakes
& on more than one continent & I've spent
    Weeks in those quaint intolerable inns
Stashed here & there in the countryside
    All around the world
But the place I keep coming back to
    My favorite of them all
Is *this* motel   the one I first came to
    Years ago stumbling down the back
Streets of Winnemucca until I found—
    June's Heavenly Motel & Motor Court
The salvation of a few wayward men
    & at least one wind-blown exhausted boy

So now I'm back again & again who knows
 How long I'll have to stay
Before it seems right once more to leave
 Maybe it's the bar here
That I love most   the chipped ceramic
 Peacocks strutting back & forth
On the treadmill June switches on every
 Night at 11 or so   or maybe
It's the white stucco walls of each unit
 With those roofs of red Spanish tile
The deep emerald doors & window frames
 & the porches all lined with baby
Palm trees   or white roses   or maybe what
 I love more is the old step-up bath
The floors & walls tiled with octagonal pieces
 The size of silver dollars
Each bluer than heaven   bluer than ice
 Even the furniture looks right off
The set of *To Have and Have Not*
 Over-stuffed chairs & rattan tables
Well   I don't know   but when I need to take
 Some time & I have nowhere else to go
I always come back here   here
 Tonight   walking back to my room
With a bucket of ice & a bottle of gin
 I figure I couldn't be doing
Much better   so I turn on the swamp cooler
 Nix the lights & strip down to nothing
In the damp black summer air
 I sit back against the bed's headboard
Holding my glass up to the window
 Where the reflection of June's neon sign
Is flashing on-&-off   on-&-off
 I pour the gin over the snapping ice
Aiming for the lime I know
 Is hunched at the bottom of the glass
& I start to wonder when it was
 That I began to throw in the towel

Before I was asked   as it starts in on me
    Again   that awful music of the conscience
& like any man who thinks he carries
    His real life in his mind
Or in his suitcase   I was worthless to
    The woman I married who was still
A child & worthless also to the child
    The daughter I carried
On my shoulders   the rider of a horse
    More wild than either she or I could ever
Have imagined & soon to be more broken
    Sitting alone at nights on the front porch
Watching the lights of the Texaco station
    Go out at 2 A.M. & after that just a
Future of no address no past just a life of
    Marginal destinations
Or once in a while a stop here at June's
    & tonight   on a mirror the size
Of a book I pour out a small mound of crystal
    Methedrine   umber flakes catching
The light outside like shattered quartz
    & with a razor I cut the flakes
To powder then draw the powder with the razor's
    Edge into six thin lines along
The mirror   my own personal *I Ching*
    & with a rolled dollar bill
I finish off each line & with a damp
    Finger clean the silver glossy mirror
Then I lean back against the pillows
    & press my right foot against
The metal rail at the bed's end & I push
    Down & push down as if it were
The pedal of the accelerator in an old truck
    Until my blood laced with methedrine
Lets me feel the way the wind is pouring
    Through the cab's open windows
As the night streaks by   as I speed towards
    A horizon stitched with moonlight

& once again all the broken gauges hanging
  Before me in the darkness
Each as white as the face of a moon
  & all the needles begin to rise slowly
Together   black arms raised at the midnight
  Erect & stiff   each needle pointing
Me on towards some more lasting & final horizon
  One as familiar as the broken white
Line of birds against
                    the black September sky

from *Green Mountains Review*

Valentino's Hair

◇   ◇   ◇

1960—my father cannot help but tell

It's been almost thirty-five years.
I can scarcely believe it, niña.
Time trusts no one and so it disappears
before us like the smoke from my cigarette.
In 1925 I was young, I was a part
of a world eating at its own edges
without being satisfied.
The Roaring Twenties didn't roar.
They swelled with passions.
They danced, and I danced with them.

I had a barber shop in a Manhattan hotel.
It is not there anymore.
It burned down during World War II.
But in its time it was elegant, private.
My shop was small, only one chair.
Every comb, every lotion, every towel perfect:
like the stars which burn in the sky,
everything shined.
The barber chair was gold-leafed
and made of the softest leather.
A man could fall asleep in that chair
with lather still fresh on his face.
There were four large oval mirrors,
two on one wall, two on the opposite wall.

They faced each other like distant lovers,
never permitted to kiss,
only permitted to greet each other
with their cool but receptive stares.

The walls had cloth wallpaper.
The wallpaper too had gold leaf
with a blue and brown background of leaves
and trees and ocean in the distance.
And it reminded me of my town Aguadilla,
the great stretches of beach,
the lush rain forests of Puerto Rico.
Anyway, fate had been good to me,
and I was owner of the barber shop
in the hotel, and I made good money,
and the times looked good,
and I lost a lot of money
before the Twenties were gone.
But that's not why I'm telling you this.

One day in 1926, early afternoon, 1:00 P.M.,
things were slow, and I was reading the paper,
studying the horse racing sheet.
Mangual had come by, picked up a couple of bets
from me and got a haircut.
He had hair in those days.
It was just after he had left,
and I remember thinking what a hot summer
we were having, and I was tipped back
in my barber chair,
almost sleeping, almost dreaming.
You know how it is when you're between
sleep and dream and a slight push
can send you into one world or the other.
Well, suddenly the wall phone rang.
I thought for sure it was Mangual.
Sometimes he'd call and try to get me
to change my bets. He'd tell me

I was wasting my money,
and he had a tip on a horse
so fast you'd think it had six legs.
The phone rang a second time.
I did not hurry. I don't quite know why,
but I waited until the fourth ring
and snapped forward in the chair
and lifted the phone receiver off the hook.
The front desk at the hotel was calling.
A guest wanted a haircut and shave.
I had no customers in the shop, except
maybe a fly seeking decay in summer heat.
I said I was available, asked for the room number.
That was that. Just another customer,
I remember thinking. Possibly a stockbroker,
a businessman, maybe Mafia.
I'd given them haircuts and shaves too.

I took my best tools.
I had recently purchased them
and had a special black leather box made.
Like a doctor.
In a way I was a kind of doctor.
What I did helped people ride a stream
to slow recovery, to arrive on the shore
of something new, something hidden.
A secret place. A secret person.
Well, so I went. I closed my shop,
putting a note on the door saying
I'd be back in an hour, and then I strutted down
the wine-red carpeted hallway into the lobby,
past the front desk and into the elevator.
I pressed the button for the eighth floor
and rode up alone to my destiny.

There was a small mirror on the elevator wall,
just above the button panel.
It was there for the ladies and gentlemen,

on their way to parties,
to look one last time at the present.
And so I did. I stared into the face
of a twenty-seven-year-old man
who knew little about the ways of this world.
And for that moment I thought I saw someone else.
Someone who was walking towards me
from another place we held in common.
The elevator door opened
to wake me from my daydream.

Room 808 was my customer,
and I found myself at the door
tapping lightly on its face.
The rooms were spacious,
and the windows faced Central Park.
I could hear the sound of an electric fan
as the door opened, and I was greeted
by a fair-haired, frail-looking man.
He was in a dark suit,
and he was smoking a cigarette in a holder.
Quite a dandy. He greeted me warmly,
thanked me for being so prompt.
His employer was absolutely desperate
to be ready for an evening engagement
and had little time or desire to walk
the busy streets looking for a barber shop,
and if he did walk the streets,
he probably would be mobbed by admirers,
and he would definitely make my time worthwhile,
and I had come highly recommended.

Well, all these things came quickly
out of this amiable, high-strung American
as he led me to a room where the light was good
and which had been prepared
with a chair, table, and large mirror.
The sink was to the left of the table.

I began setting the tools on the table
and emptying my satchel of hair and skin products,
which I had also brought with me.
As I did, I looked up at the mirror,
more so to see if it was clean than anything else.
When I did, I saw the reflection,
a dark-haired man in the mirror
standing in the doorway behind me.
It was the ladykiller.
It was Rudolph Valentino.
He looked drawn and tired.
He had obviously not shaved
for his face was already darkening with whiskers.
He was wearing a very white undershirt
and a pair of dark pants.
By his side was a very slim, exotic looking woman.
They were arguing, but very quietly,
in whispers like lovers separated
by a thin wall from their neighbors.
The woman kept insisting on something,
and she called him Rudy.
He finally looked at me staring at him
in the mirror and smiled slightly, stopping the woman
in her sentence by simply saying, "Enough!"
He closed the door behind him, walked towards me,
his hand out to shake my hand.

And to my surprise he said my name.
"I'm glad to meet you, Señor Sapia."
The look of amazement must have been on my face.
I suddenly began to feel flushed.
In the mirror I could see how red my cheeks were.
And then he apologized and told me
his secretary had a bad habit
of never informing people who their customer was.
One time in California
he needed a manicure and a pedicure.
The hotel sent up an elderly lady

to give him what he requested.
But she was never told who her client was.
When Valentino walked out to greet her,
his pants leg rolled up, barefoot,
the woman drew in a long hard look
and fainted on the royal blue rug,
her silver hair perfectly in place.
Valentino tried to revive her
and members of his party called
for the house doctor and all was panic.
And the strange thing was
they couldn't revive her.
They declared the woman dead,
Valentino concluded, remorse in his voice.
The hotel cooperated,
reported the woman died of a heart attack
in the hallway, not Valentino's room.
He had enough of scandal.
This would have been too cruel,
too bizarre, he confessed.
I was struck by Valentino's story.
Why should he tell me,
Facundo Sapia, a simple barber?

My girl, I was suddenly caught
between laughing and crying.
The poor man had a power
he couldn't control,
and here I was absolving him
of his sin, listening to his confession
like a priest in my white smock.
And now he was to do penance,
he was to give something up to me.
I would raise my chalice of shaving cream
and lift my silver razor to the light.

"Sapia means wisdom, doesn't it?" he asked.
"Yes," I told him. "My mother's name was Inocencia."
"Ah," he said. "What a beautiful name, Innocent Wisdom."
And he sat down in the chair,
looked into the mirror, and asked me
to help him with this man in the mirror,
meaning, of course, himself.
I covered him with the white apron.
And I began to apply the shaving cream
to his face while his eyes stared directly
into the eyes of the pitiful man
he thought he saw in the mirror.
I began to lather and disguise
that perfect face, slowly, with compliance,
like an accomplice to the development
of the belief in one god.
Perhaps her god was what
the elderly lady thought she saw
before she fainted into death.

As I shaved Rudolph Valentino,
he remained silent, and I remained silent.
My hands had to be steady,
for they guided the instrument
and I simply followed.
Valentino noticed my hands.
They looked like his father's hands,
the way the fingers naturally curved
when the hand relaxed.
I began to cut his hair;
he trained his eyes on my hands.
"You do not realize it," he said,
"but you are cutting away at my life too,
time leaving me like moments
falling to the floor."

Suddenly, I was afraid of a man
I could easily destroy
with one swerve of my razor,
with one jolt of my scissors.
A man who was a great lover,
not philosopher.
I didn't want to hear philosophy.
I wanted to know about the desert at night,
the ride of the four horsemen,
the posture of the tango.
But he was speaking about death,
his own death.
And he was implicating me.
But most frightening of all,
I had this disturbing feeling he was right.
He was dying. I was dying.
We were all dying at this moment,
in this place, where his hair fell calmly
to the floor like our simple desires.

Somehow I gathered my courage
and told him he had something
all men wished they had.
It was not his money or his appearance.
He immediately turned directly to me,
causing my scissor to glance
slightly off of his left ear.
He just stared at me.
Didn't say one word.
He just looked and looked into my face.
I felt like a broken fish under the eye of God;
he was waiting for the answer.
What he had was a way with women.
I told him about the woman I was in love with
but who did not even care if I lived or died.
She did not even know I existed.
Oh, she was a friend of a friend,
and we talked, but I could sense

she had no fascination for me.
It was odd to tell this to Rudolph Valentino,
a man never scorned by a woman,
a man who had probably made love
to every woman he touched.

Well, we continued in silence.
I trimming his hair,
which was in need of a haircut,
and he turned toward the mirror,
staring into his own eyes,
then once or twice stealing
a quick, deliberate glance at me.
The silence in the room
made everything else around us so loud.
My scissors clipping steadily.
The car horns from down on the street.
Suddenly I could hear the young man
and the exotic looking woman
in the next room arguing,
at first with quick exchanges and long pauses.
Then their voices grew more intense, more hateful,
until finally I heard a crash or a fall,
I really wasn't sure which.
But I could hear someone crying and gasping
and trying to talk, trying to defend.
It was the young man's voice.
I think she had hit him with something.
Valentino's eyes changed.
"Damn it, damn it," he started saying.
"Yes, I'm lucky," he said to me,
"and I'll probably be lucky in hell too."

He suddenly laughed, as if he realized
something ridiculous
far beyond his reach,
distant as his past.
By then I had begun putting talcum powder

around his neck, ready to remove
the white apron covered with his hair.
His image in the mirror was the image
I had seen in the dark theatre.
Valentino gave the mirror his famous profile,
the delicate ears, the high forehead, the angular nose.
"Señor Sapia," he said, very conclusively,
"your reputation is not exaggerated."
With that, he gave me a one hundred dollar bill
from a money clip he had in his pocket,
and he walked ceremoniously out the door.

Something happened to me, mi muchacha.
Something seized my senses.
He had said it himself:
"You are cutting away at my life too."
We all take something from each other.
It was then I got down on my knees,
began gathering with these hands his hair,
hurrying like a mad man,
afraid someone would open the door, catch me,
afraid someone would see my uncontrollable frenzy.
One month later he died and I discovered
the magical power of the hair.
It was then when I used that power.
I used it to seduce a woman I loved.
The woman who didn't love me.

from *The Reaper*

Trappings

◇ ◇ ◇

Carol and I headed for the Blues Rock Bar—walking, or more likely,
wiggling, slightly, in our three-inch platform shoes—
just as the lights in the capitol's cupola were coming on
and the floodlights were spotting the grounds,
those petunias bordering the stairs and the Midwestern grass,
already splotchy from June's scorching heat.

We made our way down State Street, stopping before the boutiques,
as they were beginning to be called, and eyeing the windows
of *Sassafras, The Peacock,* and *Compared to What,*
our favorite shoe store with its brick walls recently blasted clean—
now a flat red matting for the center display:
ruby-red boots we dreamed of pulling over our skinny calves

and showing off below our short denim skirts, one of *The Peacock*'s
western-styled blouses completing the perfect outfit. Instead,
we wore tube tops, wrinkling, slightly, beneath our small breasts
and belled jeans tight enough for the seams to lift our lips. So,
we were already divided before we entered the basement light,
bright at first, because the roadies were still setting up,

carting large round cases that looked as if they might contain
the elaborate, decorative hats of another age altogether,
like Jane Austen's, when high-crowned bonnets were trimmed
with the dyed plumes of ostrich or egret, or, broad satin ribbons,
big fat bows, a tumble of flowers, lilacs and jonquils and roses,
or, instead, a poplin cornucopia of shiny wooden fruit:

tiny hand-painted cherries; feathery strawberries; dewy
glistening plums; and, of course, when the carriage bearing
the hats had rolled up the red brick drive leading to the manor,
Austen's young ladies would have come racing over the slate stoop
and excitedly assembled, their muslin gowns of pink or green
or white—some sprigged or tamboured—all crisp as paper,

as fresh new bills, the way money begins, thin and spotless:
even the somewhat crumpled cash that Carol and I handed over
for our bottles of Pabst, the beer with the blue-ribbon labels
we scraped away with our thumbnails, rolling the tiny scraps
into missiles and flicking them off the table, often aiming
for the lighted face of the bar clock, but hitting,

instead, the thickly-postered wall that, later, they might
lean against, the ones who would ask us to go home with them:
the drummer, the roadie, or just a regular, probably,
shepherding us easily to that familiar place
where the split was confirmed by that quick, necessary act
spurred by the fantasies of such love and all its gear.

from *Shenandoah*

The Lost Golf Ball

◊ ◊ ◊

Part of the universe is missing
Sings or says the newspaper, and I believe it.
Even most of it. As tape runs out of a typewriter. Big surprise:
And it won't do to go looking for holes
Or changes in the constitution of matter
Like a rare jewel in a crossword puzzle
Or yourself as an answer
Linking and locking up space
In the accidental field where you stumble
Like a star lost on a white ceiling
Parts of the universe are missing
The random minor stars you improvised
Litter the mind but might not go out
Damned to hell not what are you but
Where are you my poem
Nothing is left but the recantation
The repetition in a glut
Miraculous as evil
Joining the democracy of pain as if to improve it
A woman like Venice and like Venetian blinds
Opening and closing
Part of the universe is missing. Missing!

Is this our bedroom or a planetarium?

The title could be an inducement like a lost ball
though it never appears in the final painting
though anything might, a buried ship, the title is a nude
but the title is not a can opener or a handle for a pot
Sometimes what is lost does make an appearance however
taking a common revenge like a word
Losing the lost golf ball, find the lost golf ball
The title itself is a ceiling for
stars that shine at night, will not fade, and stick by themselves
like a slogan
"You have made my room a universe," as you said you would

from *House (Blown Apart)*

Tennyson

◇ ◇ ◇

Like many of us he was rather disgusting,
With his deliberate dirtiness, his myopia, his smell,
His undying enmity for unfavorable reviewers,
His stinginess, his coy greed for titles, money, and gowns,
His contempt for Cockneys and Americans—
Sallow, greasy, handsome, the ur-Victorian.
Stupid, as Auden called him.

And yet one of the great songsters of the English word,
Though we still say, a century beyond,
With qualifications.
                          And modern!
A family riddled with drugs, alcohol, and insanity,
His major themes all givens or hand-me-downs,
The omnium-gatherum of "In Memoriam"
For beloved Arthur, the high-school "Idylls,"
The triumph of Faulknerian "Maud"
(Though only Browning could call it great);

Yanking his son out of Cambridge to be his biographer,
The slavey wife he truly cherished,
His fear of Darwin, his desperation for everlastingness.

Beautiful tedious Alfred, nicotine drooling from his
   meerschaum pipe,
Which he invited guests to suck,
Long-lived, the very image of English Poet,

Whose songs still break out tears in the generations,
Whose prosody for practitioners still astounds,
Who crafted his life and letters like a watch.

from *The New Yorker*

CHARLES SIMIC

The White Room

◇   ◇   ◇

The obvious is difficult
To prove. Many prefer
The hidden. I did, too.
I listened to the trees.

They had a secret
Which they were about to
Make known to me—
And then didn't.

Summer came. Each tree
On my street had its own
Scheherazade. My nights
Were a part of their wild

Storytelling. We were
Entering dark houses,
Always more dark houses,
Hushed and abandoned.

There was someone with eyes closed
On the upper floors.
The fear of it, and the wonder,
Kept me sleepless.

The truth is bald and cold,
Said the woman
Who always wore white.
She didn't leave her room.

The sun pointed to one or two
Things that had survived
The long night intact.
The simplest things,

Difficult in their obviousness.
They made no noise.
It was the kind of day
People described as "perfect."

Gods disguising themselves
As black hairpins, a hand-mirror,
A comb with a tooth missing?
No! That wasn't it.

Just things as they are,
Unblinking, lying mute
In that bright light—
And the trees waiting for the night.

from *Western Humanities Review*

The People Next Door

◇   ◇   ◇

He isn't a religious man.
So instead of going to church
on Sunday they go to sea.

They cruise up and down,
see the ferry coming from Bridgeport
to Green Harbor, and going back
from Green Harbor to Bridgeport . . .
and all the boats there are.
The occasional silent fisherman . . .
When the kids start to get restless
he heads back to shore.

I hear them returning
worn out and glad to be home.
This is as close to being happy
as a family ever gets.
I envy their content. And yet
I've done that too, and know
that no hobby or activity
distracts one from thinking
forever. Every human being
is an intellectual more or less.

I too was a family man.
It was a phase I had to go through.
I remember tenting in the Sierras,
getting up at dawn to fly cast.

I remember my young son
almost being blown off the jetty
in Oban. Only the suitcase
he was carrying held him down.
The same, at Viareggio,
followed me into the sea
and was almost swept away by the current.

These are the scenes I recall
rather than Christmas and Thanksgiving.
My life as the father of a family
seems to have been a series
of escapes, not to mention illnesses,
confrontations with teachers,
administrators, police.
Flaubert said, "They're in the right,"
looking at a bourgeois family,
and then went back happily
to his dressing gown and pipe.

Yes, I believe in the family . . .
next door. I rejoice
at their incomings and outgoings.
I am present when Betty
goes out on her first date.
I hear about Joey's being chosen
for the team. I survive the takeover
of the business, and the bad scare
at the doctor's.
I laugh with them that laugh
and mourn with them that mourn.

I see their lights, and hear a murmur
of voices, from house to house.

It gives me a strange feeling
to think how far they've come
from some far world to this,
bending their necks to the yoke
of affection.

    And that one day,
with a few simple words
and flowers to keep them company
they'll return once more to the silence
out there, beyond the stars.

   from *Poetry*

The Memory of Cock Robin Dwarfs W.D.

◊ ◊ ◊

—after the painting by DeLoss McGraw

"Each single wing-
èd thing
is terrible," said Rilke who
had known a few.
Brahms, too:

"You can't know how
even now
our ears ring with that fellow's strong
wingbeat and song."
We long,

like Semelé,
to see
what held us close only last night,
but in pure light
our sight,

fired and refined,
goes blind.
Too much of sounds we yearn to hear
can numb the ear;
that dear-

ly lovèd throat's
          charged notes
can overload our circuits, thrill
      and fuse the will
          they kill

      then, when they're gone,
          ring on.
Still, if that voice that overjoyed
      me were destroyed,
          the void

      would make me shrink
          to think
and never shape one note or word
      to match that bird
          once heard.

from *Michigan Quarterly Review*

Building

◊   ◊   ◊

We started our house midway through the Cultural Revolution,
The Vietnam war, Cambodia, in our ears,
  tear gas in Berkeley,
Boys in overalls with frightened eyes, long matted hair, ran
  from the police.
We peeled trees, drilled boulders, dug sumps, took sweat baths
  together.
That house finished we went on
Built a schoolhouse, with a hundred wheelbarrows,
  held seminars on California paleo-indians during lunch.
We brazed the Chou dynasty form of the character "Mu"
  on the blacksmithed brackets of the ceiling of the lodge,
Buried a five-prong vajra between the schoolbuildings
  while praying and offering tobacco.
Those buildings were destroyed by a fire, a pale copy rebuilt
  by insurance.

Ten years later we gathered at the edge of a meadow.
The cultural revolution is over, hair is short,
  the industry calls the shots in the Peoples Forests.
Single mothers go back to college to become lawyers.

Blowing the conch, shaking the staff-rings
  we opened work on a Hall,
Forty people, women carpenters, child labor, pounding nails,

Screw down the corten roofing and shape the beams
   with a planer,
The building is done in three weeks.
We fill it with flowers and friends and open it up to our hearts.

Now in the year of the Persian Gulf,
Of Falsehoods and Crimes in the Government held up as Virtues,
   this dance with Matter
Goes on: our buildings are solid, to live, to teach, to sit,
To sit, to know for sure the sound of a bell—

This is history. This is outside of history.
Buildings are built in the moment,
   they are constantly wet from the pool
      that renews all things
   naked and gleaming.

The moon moves
Through her twenty-eight nights.
Wet years and dry years pass;
Sharp tools, good design.

from *Witness*

Sunday Afternoon at Fulham Palace

◇ ◇ ◇

Putney Bridge, London

A Sunday afternoon in late September, one of the last
good weekends before the long dark, old couples
taking the air along the Thames, sunning themselves,
their arms and legs so pale, *exposed*,
eyes closed against the slanting autumn light,
while the young press forward, carry us
along in the crowd to the fair at Fulham Palace
where a few people have already spread blankets and tablecloths
for the picnics they've brought, laughing and talking.
as they wait for the music to begin at three o'clock.
Inside the palace gates, a man inflates
a room-size, brightly painted rubber castle,
the children impatiently waiting for walls and turrets to go up,
the spongy floor they like to jump on.
The palace is empty. The Bishop gone.
Now overfed goldfish swim slowly round and round
in the crumbling courtyard fountain, and farther on,
a white peacock stands still as a statue,
still as a stone, whether as in pride or sorrow
at being the last of its kind here I don't know.
A low door opens into the Bishop's walled garden, but once
inside nothing miraculous or forbidden tempts us,

just a few flowers and herbs among weeds
(unlike those illuminated scenes in books of hours),
the past passing away too quickly to catch or recognize.

Out on the other side, we pick our way
among booths put up for the day,
one woman, predictably, passing out pamphlets
on nuclear winter and cruise missiles, as if she could stop it alone.
The Fulham Band takes its place on the platform,
the conductor announcing as the overture
"Those Magnificent Men in Their Flying Machines,"
the crossed shadow of coincidence, of airplanes from Gatwick
passing over at two-minute intervals, touching us
for a moment before they fly into the day's
unplanned pattern of connections, the music
attracting more of a crowd, men, women, and children
making their entrances like extras in a movie,
in pairs, in families, no one alone that I can see
except one girl, no more than ten,
lagging behind the others, lost completely
in a vivid, invisible daydream until her mother finds her,
brings her back with a touch on the arm,
and the daughter says, unbelievably,
"I was thinking about what kind of anesthesia
they'll give me when I have my first baby."

The future expands, then contracts, like an eye's iris opening
    and closing,
walling me into a room where light and sound come and go,
first near, then far, as if I had vertigo.
It is easy, too easy, to imagine the world ending
on a day like today, the sun shining and the band playing,
the players dreamily moving now into Ellington's "Mood Indigo."
Easy to see the great gray plane hovering briefly overhead,
the gray metal belly opening and the bomb dropping,
a flash, a light "like a thousand suns,"
and then the long winter.
The white peacock. Erased. The goldfish in the fountain

swimming crazily as the water boils up around them, evaporates.
The children's castle. Gone. The children. The mothers and the
        fathers.
As if a hand had suddenly erased a huge blackboard.
Thank God you don't know what I'm thinking.
You press my hand as if to ask, "Am I here with you?
Do you want to go?" pulling me back to this moment,
to this music we are just coming to know, the crowd around us
growing denser, just wanting to live their lives,
each person a *nerve*, thinking and feeling
too much as sensation pours over them
in a ceaseless flow, the music, as we move to go,
jumping far back in time, the conductor oddly choosing
something devotional, a coronet solo
composed, and probably played here, by Purcell three centuries ago.
All is as it was as we make our way back along the Thames
to Putney Bridge, the old souls still sleeping unaware,
hands lightly touching, as the river bends in a gentle arc
around them. Mood indigo. The white peacock.
The walled garden and the low door.
As if, if it did happen, we could bow our heads
and ask, once more, to enter that innocent first world.

from *The Iowa Review*

WILLIAM STAFFORD

Last Day

◇ ◇ ◇

Finally rain gives the blessing. It anoints
leaves with a fine mist on the windward side,
and with tentative touches unrolls the sheen of its mild
passing. No face is neglected; all receive
a share of that vast impartial good fortune.

And some brought to that gift a gift of their own,
a gaze like a pool in the woods that waits, a depth.
And not only the rain comes—another universe
trembles forth, touched then forgotten again,
but waiting for a better time, a dawn that's forever.

from *The Ohio Review*

Reading the Facts about Frost in The Norton Anthology

◇   ◇   ◇

"Lover's quarrel" hah.
Little domestic
Eichmann in puttees
claiming he simply
had a taste for spats.

This was a real Scrooge.
His son killed himself.
Wait till you hear what
Mr. Thompson told
Mr. Ellmann. That's

all I know and all
I need to know. Frost
was a pig to his
wife, children, colleagues
and biographer.

So don't get suckered,
undergraduates.
Like by the poems.
Like by sycophants
or apologists.

We can instruct you
also about the
Galápagos: "an
island group in
the Caribbean."

from *Poetry*

Movie

◇ ◇ ◇

Not quite sleep, but nearly all we want of it—
These dreams framed in the metal of what's real,
a silence perfected by voices, the smoky erotic twilight
when the houselights dim and the world emerges
en négligé and as it moves toward us, through gauzy blue,
we glimpse its nudity in the form of stories; when we live here,
everything we want to happen does, without becoming history.
A miracle, isn't it? This photography of what we feel.
That undetected murder in the mind, the inner burglary
just foiled as the waiter brings two orders of cassis sorbet,
the wish to sleep with so-and-so, are being filmed.
The black car as it plunges inevitably
from the cliff, encodes regret, all that cannot be relived;
with just that open mouth, those outstretched arms, we call out to
        what falls
beyond recovery:
Elsewhere, the Ming-necked girl gripped by the steely gangster
warns that love and beauty are always in danger.

To be adult and still unborn is one kind of ideal.
Here attention's prenatal, velvet, wall-to-wall,
and life's doubled, flesh is flesh's symbol,
a jewel worn on the wrist and in the eye,
diamond in day, diamond again in dream,
the best thing yet we've fashioned from the dark,
these angels of our thought on screen;

we watch them raptly as we watch our dead,
the little candles of remembered gestures lit,
loved features we live by, again and again. Again. Again.

from *The New York Review of Books*

MARK STRAND

Reading in Place

◇ ◇ ◇

Imagine a poem that starts with a couple
Looking into a valley, seeing their house, the lawn
Out back with its wooden chairs, its shady patches of green,
Its wooden fence, and beyond the fence the rippled silver sheen
Of the local pond, its far side a tangle of sumac, crimson
In the fading light. Now imagine somebody reading the poem
And thinking, "I never guessed it would be like this,"
Then slipping it into the back of a book while the oblivious
Couple, feeling nothing is lost, not even the white
Streak of a flicker's tail that catches their eye, nor the slight
Toss of leaves in the wind, shift their gaze to the wooded dome
Of a nearby hill where the violet spread of dusk begins,
But the reader, out for a stroll in the autumn night, with all
The imprisoned sounds of nature dying around him, forgets
Not only the poem, but where he is, and thinks instead
Of a bleak Venetian mirror that hangs in a hall
By a curving stair, and how the stars in the sky's black glass
Sink down and the sea heaves them ashore like foam.
So much is adrift in the ever-opening rooms of elsewhere,
He cannot remember whose house it was, or when he was there.
Now imagine he sits years later under a lamp
And pulls a book from the shelf; the poem drops
To his lap. The couple are crossing a field
On their way home, still feeling that nothing is lost,
That they will continue to live harm-free, sealed
In the twilight's amber weather. But how will the reader know,

Especially now that he puts the poem, without looking,
Back in the book, the book where a poet stares at the sky
And says to a blank page, "Where, where in Heaven am I?"

from *Grand Street*

Harvest, 1925

◇ ◇ ◇

It took two nights to shuck the Hawfields' corn,
  piled, foreskinned, altar high,
    outside the crib.
Lanternlight. Hard trolling motions.
  Dark pent-up communion.
    With supper first, many
women together, in church clothes
  preparing food relentlessly
    as if for some dread rite.
Big Helen Hawfields
  (her long sultry breasts,
    her deep unwilling laugh)
stalked the harvest table
  lost out the window in
    the high encroaching winter wind,
the empty calyxes
  of cotton, a spinster's net—(o
    do not let the world depart
nor close thine eyes against the night)—
  she filled the lanterns
    trembling, the long wicks heavy
with combustible,
  all the blurred brandy dreams
    in her outskirts
gathering in one drunk longing for
  Tattoo's broad body.
    Below the shuck pile

was a paradise
    lipped by wild plums
        in troubled tangle;
his Maggie found them there,
    stood, hard-cheeked, dazed
        at Tattoo's gnashing grin—back
to the mourners' bench!—
    at Helen's bent-up scuttering,
        weeping, behind the plums,
a lactate field mouse,
    shucks cleaving
        to her teats.

from *The Seneca Review*

Trust Me

◊ ◊ ◊

Who did I write last night? leaning
over this yellow pad, here, inside,
making blue chicken tracks: two
sets of blue footprints, tracking out
on a yellow ground,
child's colors.

Who am I?
who want so much to move
like a fish through water,
through life . . .
                    Fish *like* to be
underwater.

Fish move through fish! Who
are you?

And Trust Me said, There's another way to go,
we'll go by the river which is frozen under the snow;

my shining, your shining life draws close, draws closer,
God fills us as a woman fills a pitcher.

from *Boulevard*

RICHARD WILBUR

Lying

◇ ◇ ◇

To claim, at a dead party, to have spotted a grackle
When in fact you haven't of late, can do no harm.
Your reputation for saying things of interest
Will not be marred, if you hasten to other topics,
Nor will the delicate web of human trust
Be ruptured by that airy fabrication.
Later, however, talking with toxic zest
Of golf, or taxes, or the rest of it
Where the beaked ladle plies the chuckling ice,
You may enjoy a chill of severance, hearing
Above your head the shrug of unreal wings.
Not that the world is tiresome in itself:
We know what boredom is: it is a dull
Impatience or a fierce velleity,
A champing wish, stalled by our lassitude,
To make or do. In the strict sense, of course,
We invent nothing, merely bearing witness
To what each morning brings again to light:
Gold crosses, cornices, astonishment
Of panes, the turbine-vent which natural law
Spins on the grill-end of the diner's roof,
Then grass and grackles or, at the end of town
In sheen-swept pastureland, the horse's neck
Clothed with its usual thunder, and the stones
Beginning now to tug their shadows in
And track the air with glitter. All these things
Are there before us; there before we look

225

Or fail to look; there to be seen or not
By us, as by the bee's twelve thousand eyes,
According to our means and purposes.
So too with strangeness not to be ignored,
Total eclipse or snow upon the rose,
And so with that most rare conception, nothing.
What is it, after all, but something missed?
It is the water of a dried-up well
Gone to assail the cliffs of Labrador.
There is what galled the arch-negator, sprung
From Hell to probe with intellectual sight
The cells and heavens of a given world
Which he could take but as another prison:
Small wonder that, pretending not to be,
He drifted through the bar-like boles of Eden
In a *black mist low creeping*, dragging down
And darkening with moody self-absorption
What, when he left it, lifted and, if seen
From the sun's vantage, seethed with vaulting hues.
Closer to making than the deftest fraud
Is seeing how the catbird's tail was made
To counterpoise, on the mock-orange spray,
Its light, up-tilted spine; or, lighter still,
How the shucked tunic of an onion, brushed
To one side on a backlit chopping-board
And rocked by trifling currents, prints and prints
Its bright, ribbed shadow like a flapping sail.
Odd that a thing is most itself when likened:
The eye mists over, basil hints of clove,
The river glazes toward the dam and spills
To the drubbed rocks below its crashing cullet,
And in the barnyard near the sawdust-pile
Some great thing is tormented. Either it is
A tarp torn loose and in the groaning wind
Now puffed, now flattened, or a hip-shot beast
Which tries again, and once again, to rise.
What, though for pain there is no other word,
Finds pleasure in the cruellest simile?

It is something in us like the catbird's song
From neighbor bushes in the grey of morning
That, harsh or sweet, and of its own accord,
Proclaims its many kin. It is a chant
Of the first springs, and it is tributary
To the great lies told with the eyes half-shut
That have the truth in view: the tale of Chiron
Who, with sage head, wild heart, and planted hoof
Instructed brute Achilles in the lyre,
Or of the garden where we first mislaid
Simplicity of wish and will, forgetting
Out of what cognate splendor all things came
To take their scattering names; and nonetheless
That matter of a baggage-train surprised
By a few Gascons in the Pyrenees
Which, having worked three centuries and more
In the dark caves of France, poured out at last
The blood of Roland, who to Charles his king
And to the dove that hatched the dove-tailed world
Was faithful unto death, and shamed the Devil.

from *New and Collected Poems*

227

ALAN WILLIAMSON

The Muse of Distance

◇   ◇   ◇

What composes a life? Mine comes, too much, from books;
but also the sense that, if you climbed high places,

you would see the streets go on with nothing to end them,
and be driven to, perhaps even desire,

whatever they withheld: a flight of smokestacks past water;
a girl in a mean, dawn-blue room; a glimpse of the terrible

engines, or giants, it took to make such a world . . .

★

Far in the caverns of our night, a jarring:
then chinks of light

at both doors to my room, and sausage-smells from our huge
travellers' breakfast; then lugging the suitcases, down

from the hiding-places where they'd kept all winter—
tribal ochre: the trademark an Indian's head

off an old penny—down the long stairwell, black
rail, white balusters, to the mirroring black-

and-white tile at the foot, not scarily dim now, but bathed
through the jewel-faceted panes

of the entrance hall beyond, in silveriness
without origin or ray . . . So our years came round, as far back

as I can remember, to this ritual of detaching
ourselves from ourselves westward:

our summer in California; half the continent's
breadth; a journey reliving

my father's childhood, failure by fresh start, westward;
which was, perhaps, why his nerves flared to get away

at seven, on schedule, so that he lashed out at
my mother or me, some wrong way I packed the trunk

or failed to make it lock—"If you grew up
the way most people do, that's what your precious

intelligence would be judged by!"—betraying not only
me, but his whole life there, with the quiet,

the high-ranged books . . . And yet the happiness,
the *Nunc Dimittis*, when we set our course down

the east-west numbered streets, half-fused with the sun risen
from the lake behind us, touching with unwitnessing strangeness

—as, back in the apartment, I had touched
the dinosaur bones on my dresser, knowing nothing

would change their position or how the light would pass them
all the days till fall—the dewy Gothic mirage

of the University; the Negro blocks; the airport's
prairie-tan lanes . . .

When we passed the garbage dump, my father marvelled
in hoots and youks, and held his nose, as if everything

he hated in his life were exposed, concentrated,
rotted and burned at once. For the next half hour—

the country coming on, meadowlarks starting
from the wet ditchgrass, but the great heat rising

more unimpeded than ever in the city—
he sang:

   You were my girl in cal-i-co,
   I was your bashful barefoot beau,
   I wrote on your slate, I love you so,
   When we were—a couple—of kids!

★

My Great-Uncle George hopped the train where it slowed
for the curve near the family farm
eight miles out of Galesburg. He'd done it often,
but this January night couldn't awaken
conductor or passengers. I can imagine
the corridor through the window, lucid, empty,
and how he managed, in the gathering speed, to unbuckle
and reloop his belt around some grip.
                    They found his
frozen body still hanging there in the gaslight
of the Chicago yards.

                I imagine my father
was named for him, whether before or after
I've no idea. In any case, they moved West
so early and repeatedly, the death
could only have followed like a kind of legend
or coat-of-arms.
           Often, crossing the Midwest,
on the new bypass skirting some blind place-name,
my father would say, "I went to high school here,"

or "we had a farm," and then "only my poor father
would have bought such land. I suppose they bailed him
out. They always did."

                        We never stopped to visit
those family places, though once we were turned away
at the Brown Palace dining room in Denver, because
I had no tie on. (I was fourteen.)
"Take a look anyway," my father said shyly,
and nudged me past a door—the wrought-iron well
above the lobby, leather sofas: "That's where
I sat and held the gold brick!"
                              —a real one;
for maybe half an hour, while Uncle Alvin
went upstairs and made his calls.

Next morning we drove out an indeterminate, elm-lined boulevard
to a lavender-Gothic house. When I got out
to take a picture, he said I was "making a spectacle";
and then, as we pulled away, "it must have been here
that I had the t.b. That bilious attic room."

And I said, "It *must*? But Daddy, don't you know?"

Then off again: but that night I wondered
just what he was revisiting when, as often,
he groaned himself to sleep.
                        (Though my mother once
returned from the thin-walled motel bathroom, her voice
a mixture of panic and triumph—"They were saying,
*'do you think there's something wrong
with that man in there?'* "
                        —it was not an
unmusical sound: long, falling, half a sigh,
like wind in the wires, or a train distancing.)

                        ★

But what I remember best are the anonymous towns
whose Main Streets we walked at twilight, drugged
with the slow lift of six-hundred-mile days
—not even stared at: as though our speed were written
like a protective mark, across our brows—
in those Main Streets still smelling of grass, or the desert's sharpness . . .

It was the things that wrenched at me the most
in those places: a dead firm's name still silver-dollared
in the cool pavement between new display windows;
and all the tools, that lived and toughened and rusted with
men's hands—the unsold harvesters shining
in the first fall light, more terrible than the graveyards
one passed on the outskirts, Indian-fringed with alders . . .

The things were like a song, that could only be heard near the earth,
only two or three inches above it: of men becoming
what they did to live; of raw skill, contempt for the mind;
or just of conditions, equal and without rancor,
of the slow flesh, that has no hope not to vanish
with all it touches . . . whispering, near the earth.

And yet if it was high summer, and the road wound
along the bluffs where the tall old scalloped houses
stood embraced by verandas, I invariably
would ask my mother, "Don't you wish we lived here?"
She would sigh, or else be drawn—*of course not, no*
theater, no art museums, no real friends—

And she was right: I didn't, really; what I loved
were the Triple A timetable cards, *Vandalia*
16 minutes, 30 minutes Centralia:
the never quite being in one place, the wind
always the same through the scarcely opened windows;

and yet being everywhere; and, as I grew older, imagining
someone waiting—as if I were called to scatter love
like a wanderer scattering apples, through death's arbitrary
stations and ends . . .

★

—When the moon moves and the bare driftwood splinters
stand out on the Nevada station wall
I close my eyes, lie on a hard bench, and see
when I am too guilty to picture you, it is you,
the scarps toward your breasts . . .

—It is last year's antlers, pointing somewhere in the mountains.

—Yes, you were always one for pointing elsewhere;
and yet there is no place you have not given.
You always lived in the only house with a tower
in the level prairie town.
Your hair was the red Southern clearing, its snakes and lianas;
your eyes a torn screen door
somewhere flashing on coolness.
The empty watery taste of motel air at day's end
is a scarf
you left behind you,
a view of weeds in new earth by a train scar.

And when we meet at the last cottonwood
going into the desert,
drawn up in the dry whisper
of her leaves on themselves
over and over,
will we spring together
into the final jewelcase of the air?

—We are lying together so far across the moonlight,
you can feel the weeds start growing through your hair.

★

233

Aunt Mary Alice always asked if the girls I liked
had auburn hair. Uncle Harold, she said, always
liked auburn-haired girls—
                    though hers was dark, darker
than the foxfur stole I loved on her, with the real
little teeth and paws, and the little tawny depthless
glass-chip eyes.

            —This was beyond the desert,
beyond the distance where America
almost floats off in the blueness between mesas
and thunderheads, an opaline shudder neither
transparence nor obstruction . . .
                        beyond that end, a city
that seemed a slightly seasick form of motion,
sea palms and mountain pines, the smell of driving,
the center always just behind you—unless

it centered, as for me, up stairs exhaling
dry stucco, in a room with carefully kept
American coin silver, the mantel clock bonging,
and a sampler with not HOME SWEET HOME but a woolly
locomotive, car, and ocean liner, and OVER
THE LAND / OVER THE SEA / TRAVELLING FAR AND WIDE.

And under it, leg raised and gauzed, no traveller
but a man cars couldn't keep from leaping onto—
off of jacks; unnoticed and unbraked in driveways—
until he had little underarm skin left to be grafted
and "take," or not, over long weeks, on his leg's
reopened tread,
                my Uncle Harold sat waiting,
eyes bulging as he talked, a rapid-fire
high harmonica twang of hyperbolic
bewilderment, that comes back a tune without words, or the broken
words of old age: how his footsteps cracked in the air
of subzero prairie mornings; how they drove a hundred miles
to pick up everyone, "out to Burbank, the big bands came there—"

A song heard near the earth, only two or three inches above it . . .

And my father listening, almost abashed, only later
shaking his head at how much he'd heard about fishing trips—
yet fond, and almost guilty; and, for all his professorial
moustache, so like his brother, their long skulls
all angles and knobs, and the hair spurting out of them
in short sparky wires—all hardness, but hardness never
at peace with itself: the expression formal, shy,
and ready to break apart in *Jeepers creepers*
haywire whimsy—like a machine some Futurist
was designing, while they walked to school, on the icy Plains.

★

What held him there in L.A.?—the mantel clock bonging
musically, with a long premonitory rasp
on the quarter hour, that, hurrying time, held it
still, unimportant, adrift . . .

My grandfather,
in the Depression—the last farm gone, the cow
sold, it was said, "so George could go to college"—
failed to see a streetcar as he came home one sunrise
from his last job, night-watchman
at a warehouse, in L.A. . . .

And all his children
lingered, except my father, already gone; and one
uncle, whom I hardly knew,
retired early, married late, and bought a trailer,
and lived, it seemed, in a kind of roving family
of trailer-couples, linking up near Christmas
in Guadalajara; in the spring, up Oregon way . . .

depthless, to us, as if he'd stepped off in that air
between mesa and cloud.

★

235

I thought I knew what Uncle Harold did. Then, once, at our place
(our summer place, in Monterey) a wall-outlet failed.

I said, "We'll have to get an electrician."
Uncle Harold said, "I am an electrician."

I said, "You're kidding. I thought you—"
                              and suddenly
I didn't quite know what I'd thought. I looked to my father,
but he just looked surprised, and said with an indefinable
hurt in his voice,
                 "Of course your Uncle Harold
is an electrician."

Harold worked for Lockheed: the intricate
circuits that held the big jets up in the sky.
But that wasn't the point: my mother and I were outsiders
on any such ground.
                Sometimes, on the trip, he'd compare
his arm with ours, where it rested, freckle-stained
as a gas station floor, on the rim of the open window—
"I can't tan the way you people do, I only burn";
or watching a home movie, after twenty years, would get angry
at the way she was standing, off by herself, in the hallway
of his parents' house.
             And one winter, in Chicago—

"I'm not going to work in the factory, after all,"
I yelled at him.

(I'd gotten a D in Phys. Ed. For two weeks, total silence
on the subject. I conferred with my mother:

"But those aren't his values. He doesn't play ball, or—"

And she: "Whatever men want for themselves, for their sons
they want the other."
               "But a professor—"

236

                                   "Just
because they're professors, they can't stop being men . . ."

—leaving me wondering just what *I* was, included
in this sad, superior, helpless, womanly
understanding . . .)

                    Now, *going to work in the factory*
hung in the lunch-table air. Then my father saying,
with deadly calm,
                    "Two of my brothers did."

I rushing in heedless, "But Daddy, you were the exception
in your family. If a professor's kid—"

He managed the worldly, world-weary smile of his prose,
feeling fused with intellect. "Oh, I know,
you're the exception—"

"I didn't say that. What I said was, *you* were—"

Then the voice of the Lord in thunder, drowning me out:

"You're the exception! You're always the exception!"

                                   ★

Two of my brothers did: it was his wish
he hated, completed in mine.

                    When Uncle Harold
failed to show up for a family reunion, or awkwardly
we had to shift at the last minute and stay
with one of my aunts—
                    As a child, I didn't notice.
Later, the explanations:

                    "He can't touch a drop now, or—"

"He was the one who went down to the morgue when our father—"

But Aunt Mary Alice, looking down at her own
arthritis-jewelled fingers,
said once, "Harold has fine hands, a surgeon's hands.
He wanted to be a doctor, but the Depression—
and 'the cow was sold for George to go to college'—"

When I told my father, he winced, as if he'd bitten
something sour, then sighed, "Harold wanted to be everything.
He was going to write a great novel, and we'd all
be famous from it. He'd make a million dollars
on the movie—"

He didn't, of course. Like my father, he gave
half his paycheck to keep their parents in their own house,
until the sunrise and the streetcar . . .

He *did his duty*, in that brontosaurian
language my father spoke more, when they'd been together,
as he laughed at jokes on "the colored"; remembered his
   Model T Ford.

★

When "the t.b." returned in him, after years
of late-night writing, slowly angrier nerves,
and he hung in the balance all summer, needing seven
times the normal dose of drugs
                —small wonder
I turned to Christ, the eternal
son, who dies a little
(or much) to live beyond his father's justice
without calling it a lie.

            I gave up my childhood anger—
its study of execution and torture, that put the iron
and smoke of Chicago winter into my soul—
in a kind of floating calm, a long June

238

dusk of forgiveness, in which the city
lay murmuring interfused, the dying
and the newly born.

                    I thought it ungodly to fear death;
though in daydreams I saw my spirit, airborne
above my body, in a hospital bed like my father's,
hover near the bowed heads, ecstatic to tell them how silly
they were not to know how simple it was—then pausing
in a white ceiling corner, not quite sure where to go.

And my father, in his loose-hanging hospital gown,
haggard, slowed down enough to be sweet and wry,
not embarrassed, at my first crush on a girl—
making me know the Mystery
was simply true: in suffering, we were reborn.

But, when he recovered, things weren't much changed. He'd still
sing, as on leaving Chicago, the last ten miles
approaching "our shanty." But when we'd actually driven
up Monterey Heights, almost to its scalplock of pines . . .

It's a scene I somehow never entirely escape from.
The fog already coming in; or perhaps not, and glare.
The earthless white granite soil and pine-needle duff.
My parents go over every inch of the house
for "the tenants'" misdoings, every vanished glass or
scratch in the varnish, as if it would tell them what
is missing from what they wanted.

                    Wherever they move, the floor gives
its slight, incurable booming reverberation
from the space too big for a crawl-space and never
finished as a cellar. My father's anger mounts,
shakes everything, ceases, each year, in no particular
proportion to what is lost.

                    I sit in my room, too visible
from the other rooms, the stucco arc of street;
and as I might think of a person—a pair of perfect,
calm, understanding eyes—think of Chicago,
where there are other people, worn gold
interiors to glimpse from the car at night, returning,
in a rush of such black, such deep-gripped-down
cottonwood trees, my own life would grip down
and sleep on itself, dark, full, opening our door
on rich books, peaceful must.

                    But that is gone
to the far side of the summer. Christ
is less a refuge. If I am not to live
a frozen ghost in the middle wind, a distance
that can never become a place, I must

be here, with them.

★

When I was fourteen I made up a sentence: *we are unhappy
because we have no roots.*
I wasn't sure of it; I'd read something like it in *Time.*
Perhaps we weren't unhappy, or *too many roots*
would have been truer . . .

                    But I know it struck on
something in me; some place where I was dreaming,
against us, an image of the true house, solid
on the solid land: the summers falling stationary
through the bay windows; piano music dampered
at night, in the thick leaves; and up the stairs
unnumbered branching alcoves, sisters, silences—

like a house in a book, where a distant lake was visible
from one upper window—enough endlessness
to rest a family in each other and
the ground beneath,

so that, if one lived there, a life
would fall like an image: first love to white stone a falling
of original leaves . . .
                    and the unseen sister upstairs
comes out and gathers it all into her hands.

That was my dream, as we passed the small towns sleeping . . .
But what my father remembered (though he could never approve
    of himself
for having arrived there) were the intimations
of a world beyond: how a store would have, from some wanderer,
almost postage-stamp-sized books, *The Ballad of Reading Gaol* or
Non Sum Qualis Eram Bonae Sub Regno Cynarae . . .

And though I said *we are unhappy, we have no roots,* I know
when I reach back as far as I can for an image
of happiness, I come to images of travel:

the DIP signs in the desert, the runningboards
and buck-tan interiors of '40s cars;
or asking my parents, in Needles, California,
one night when I was four, "How far away are the stars?"—

expecting I don't know what, a few city blocks
or even as far as L.A.—and then the vastness
of the answer somehow soothing, as our departure
soothed, back in Chicago, the dinosaur bones, the chairs . . .

We seem contented in vastness, as we do not, wholly,
anyplace solid, where our weight and distance
can be determined . . . in this, "the exception"
though we are forever, most purely American.

from *The Muse of Distance*

Madrid

◇   ◇   ◇

So the villa, having learned its many skills
through riding the bluish ochre waves of sand and clay,
has fooled us again. The moon is only a moon,
without the olive sheen and horse hoof of Granada.
No ruffled lace guitars clutch at the darkened windows.
The bilious green watermarks on old houses
only make you think of the candle wind,
gathering its hammer force season after season,
a tempered master with a gray design.
Even the wall has been undone by sierra loneliness.

Perhaps on some theatrical night,
Lope fell in love with Elena,
and acted out her virtues,
until the father bored him.
That could only end in scandalous verses,
cuffs and a ticket out of Madrid,
a cloaked night at a village gate,
a loping horse and lovers shedding
                              the acacia trees.
Better this picking at the poor brick and earth
than the bed where the mournful knight lies,
                    dreaming of dowry
                  —some household furniture,
                  an orchard, five vines, four beehives,
                  forty-five hens, one cock and a crucible—
or the Italian guile and papal star of a duke's daughter.

It is late, and the voices of Tollán swing
on the porch of the Puerta de Alcalá.
Criollos dawdle in the Plaza Mayor,
brushing the white ruff of their provincial injuries.
The Panadería has gone, with its bull blood,
autos-da-fé and saints,
and the mimetic houses sink into shadow.
And yet that dead sun has awakened
the mountain mother in the oval plaza,
and these old women in black manta scudder
over the Manzares bed,
following the lights of Taxco silver, silk,
                    Luke's virgin and a good name.

It is late,
Palm Sunday,
on a day when the mask will drop
and a slouch hat and voluminous cloak
will uncover the exiled heart.
It is late,
the May day when the sun's red heart
                    returns from its exile,
and the Emperor's horsemen fall and begin
the unraveling of a Morning Star.
It is late,
when the Queen has gone,
in gentleman's attire,
to exhibit her hunger for boar meat
and a Bourbon husband with a taste for peace.
It is late,
when the red flag of the most violent summer
calls an end to the nation's yearning.

It is time
for the jeweled humiliation of the chosen
                    to be revealed.

Now when the snow falls on this crucible
of sullen winds and interrupted passions,
there will be the dark bell sound of a mother,
crying the name she can never have,
        or having it, fulfill.

from *The Yale Review*

CONTRIBUTORS'
NOTES AND
COMMENTS

Born in Whiteville, North Carolina, in 1926, A. R. ("ARCHIE") AMMONS started writing poetry on board a United States destroyer escort in the South Pacific during the Second World War. After his return to civilian life, Ammons was in succession a science major at Wake Forest University, a graduate student in Berkeley, an elementary school principal in Cape Hatteras, and a sales executive in his father-in-law's biological glass company on the southern New Jersey shore. He has taught at Cornell University since 1964. He has received the National Book Award (1973), the Bollingen Prize (1975), the National Book Critics Circle Award (1981), and a MacArthur Fellowship. His most recent books are *The Selected Poems: Expanded Edition* and *Sumerian Vistas*, both published by Norton in 1987.

Of "Anxiety's Prosody," Ammons writes: "I remember reading somewhere—in Shakespeare, maybe—that a person under extreme anxiety tears off his or her clothes. In a state of anxiety you can't stand corporality and you want to attenuate into openness and strip away the bodily impediments. That relieves the anxiety in some way. Anxiety tries to get rid of everything thick and material—to arrive at a spiritual emptiness, the emptiness that is spiritual."

JOHN ASHBERY was born in Rochester, New York, in 1927. He is the author of twelve books of poetry, including *April Galleons* (Viking, 1987). Twice named a Guggenheim Fellow, he received the Pulitzer Prize, the National Book Award, and the National Book Critics Circle Award for his 1975 collection *Self-Portrait in a Convex Mirror* (Viking). A volume of his art criticism, *Reported Sightings*, is to be published in 1989 by Knopf. He was guest editor of *The Best American Poetry, 1988*.

$$* \qquad * \qquad *$$

BETH BENTLEY, a native of St. Paul, Minnesota, was educated at the University of Minnesota and at the University of Michigan, where she won a Hopwood Award for a novel in 1948. Her books include *Phone Calls from the Dead* (Ohio University Press, 1971), *Country of Resemblances* (Ohio University Press, 1976), *Field of Snow* (Gemini Press, 1973), *Philosophical Investigations* (SeaPen Press, 1977), and *The Purely Visible* (SeaPen Press, 1980). She teaches an evening poetry workshop for continuing education students at the University of Washington. She has lived in Seattle since 1952.

Bentley writes: " 'Northern Idylls' was written a short time after I had watched *Shoah* for four consecutive nights on PBS. As the survivors told their stories, they were often asked what month or year such and such took place. I could not help trying to recall what I was doing at each of those times—I was living a fairly innocent adolescent life in Minneapolis and, like most Jewish Americans, had only the barest idea of what was happening in Europe; our imaginations could not, at that time, even begin to comprehend the horrors. That the landscape and climate of northern Europe were so much like the country around Minneapolis reinforced my realization of unspeakable happenings. When I began to juxtapose the story of the singing boy with memories of my girlhood, the narration took the shape it has, two stories told simultaneously, one breaking into the other. This form happened spontaneously, I'm afraid, not as a premeditated device. It also expresses my idea of the 'unspeakable,' though in *Shoah*, that incredibly moving documentary, the wonder of it was that the survivors did, indeed, speak."

ELIZABETH BISHOP (1911–79) was born in Worcester, Massachusetts, grew up in New England and Nova Scotia, and was educated at Vassar College. She lived for long periods in Key West, Florida, and in Brazil. She won the Pulitzer Prize for *A Cold Spring* (1955), the National Book Award for *Questions of Travel* (1965), and the National Book Critics Circle Award for *Geography III* (1976). *The Complete Poems, 1927–1979* was published by Farrar, Straus, and

Giroux in 1983. A year later the same publisher brought out her *Collected Prose.*

The poet Lorrie Goldensohn, who discovered "It Is Marvellous . . . ," writes: "Across from me, at her dining room table, in an elegantly casual apartment in a large provincial city in Brazil, a legatee of Elizabeth Bishop held out a sheaf of papers with one hand and, smiling tentatively, pushed over a shoebox full of small notebooks with the other. She spoke no English; I spoke no Portuguese; we were entering these waters on my French, a rather fragile conveyance. But no one else had read these papers, I was sure I heard her say, since Bishop herself. They were an inheritance in English to a woman who spoke no English, who had nonetheless quietly guarded them for nearly a decade.

"I unfolded a sheet of onionskin, slightly crackling with age, buff-color now, and read through a typed, completed poem I'd never seen before, not in any of the dozens of boxes of Bishop papers currently held for scholarly use. Later, a close draft of the same poem in that small, unmistakable handwriting that looks like frayed smocking or the traffic on a much-used desk blotter turned up in a black looseleaf binder from the shoebox, positioned between other Key West poems: it was a piece probably written in the early forties."

The typescript of the poem, Ms. Goldensohn adds, is "conspicuously unadorned with any of those boxed or questioned alternative words or phrases with which the writer usually indicates unfinished work."

Lorrie Goldensohn teaches at Vassar College. She is working on a critical study of Elizabeth Bishop's poetry, for which she has received a grant from the National Endowment for the Humanities. A collection of Goldensohn's poems, *The Tether*, was published in 1982 by L'Epervier Press.

ROBERT BLY was born in Madison, Minnesota, in 1926. He graduated from Harvard in 1950. A Fulbright Fellowship took him to Norway, where he translated Scandinavian poetry and prose. In 1958 he founded and edited a poetry magazine called *The Fifties* (and later *The Sixties* and briefly *The Seventies*). His books include *The*

Light Around the Body (1967; winner of the National Book Award), *Sleepers Joining Hands* (1973), and *Selected Poems* (1986), all published by Harper & Row. His edition of *Selected Poetry and Prose of Thoreau* (Sierra Club) appeared in 1987. He lives in Moose Lake, Minnesota.

Of "My Father at 85," Robert Bly writes: "Both my father and mother had moved some years ago to a small-town nursing home where I visited them from time to time. The nurses called one day and said my father, having a mild case of pneumonia, had been moved to the hospital. When I found my father alone in the room, I sat down by his bed and wrote this poem. I had never composed a line before in his presence. For this poem I adopted the skinny lines I first experienced when translating Neruda's *Odas Elementales*."

CATHERINE BOWMAN was born in El Paso, Texas, in 1957. She grew up in San Antonio, where she worked as a journalist and graduated from the University of Texas at San Antonio in 1982. A 1988 graduate of Columbia University's M.F.A. Writing Program, she currently lives in New York and teaches writing in the public schools. Her work has appeared in *Kingfisher, The Paris Review, River Styx*, and *Webster Review*.

Of "Twins of a Gazelle Which Feed Among the Lilies," Bowman writes: "The abecedarian form, best known for its use in lamentations, prayers, alchemic incantations, and nursery books, inspired this meditation. I sat down at my desk one snowy night and copied down the alphabet in the left column of a long sheet of paper. The poem came out in a gush, each letter a clue to what should follow.

"Long after I had written the poem I heard someone say that we all have one good breast and one bad one, and I thought yes, that is what I was after."

GEORGE BRADLEY was born in Roslyn, New York, in 1953. His work has appeared in many magazines, including *Poetry, Grand Street, American Poetry Review, The Paris Review, The Yale Review, Partisan Review, Shenandoah, The New Republic, Antaeus, Spazio Umano* (Italy), and *America Illustrated*. *Terms to Be Met*, his collection of poems, was published in the Yale Series of Younger Poets in May 1986. His work appeared in the 1988 edition of *The Best American Poetry* and will be included in the forthcoming *University Press Anthology*, edited by Ron Wallace and published by the University of Wisconsin Press.

Concerning "Of the Knowledge of Good and Evil," Bradley writes: "This poem is the result of an obvious idea finally dawning upon me: that it is the knowledge of death that has brought good and evil into this world, rather than vice versa. The piece represents a recent reworking of material I first toyed with nearly ten years ago, when I lived in a factory building in Brooklyn. I used to write sitting next to a woodburning stove with my typewriter propped on a chair in front of me, and I suppose the stark circumstances might have suggested the poem's primitive setting."

DAVID BUDBILL was born into the working class in Cleveland, Ohio, in 1940. He is the author of twelve books; among them are four books of poems— *The Chain Saw Dance* (Countryman Press, 1977), *From Down to the Village* (The Ark, 1981), *Pulp Cutters' Nativity* (Countryman Press, 1981), and *Why I Came to Judevine* (White Pine Press, 1987)—that serve as the basis for his play *Judevine*. He is also the author of a novel, *Bones on Black Spruce Mountain* (Bantam, 1984), and a collection of short stories, *Snowshoe Trek to Otter River* (Bantam, 1979), for young adults. He was a Guggenheim Fellow in poetry in 1982. He lives with his wife and daughter in the remote mountains of northern Vermont, where he continues to write with one foot in the theater and the other in poetry. Most recently he has incorporated his lifelong love for improvised music into his poetry readings by using his tenor saxophone during his performances.

Of "What I Heard at the Discount Department Store," Budbill writes: "Poetry is about feeling, about being healed through feeling. Poetry is not about language. Language is a tool, a means to an end, and that end is vivid pictures, powerful emotion, musical expression—in short, cathartic emotional experience. Poetry, for me, like music, is a path to the emotional articulation of the joys and sorrows of this life, and when that articulation is good we are somehow, mysteriously, if only for a moment, transformed and healed."

*   *   *.

MICHAEL BURKARD was born in Rome, New York, in 1947. He received a B.A. from Hobart College and an M.F.A. from the University of Iowa. He has worked as a clerk, as a psychiatric aide, and as a proofreader in Bloomingdale's catalogue department; he has taught at various schools and colleges, most recently Syracuse University and Sarah Lawrence College. His poetry books include *In a White Light* (L'Epervier Press, 1977), *Ruby for Grief* (University of Pittsburgh, 1981), *The Fires They Kept* (Metro Book Co., 1986), and *Fictions from the Self* (W. W. Norton, 1988). *My Secret Boat*, a book of poems and prose memoir, will be published by W. W. Norton in 1990. He is married to the painter Mary Alice Johnston.

Burkard writes: "I wrote 'Hotel Tropicana' while traveling on a bus near Philadelphia in 1986. I was traveling frequently that winter by bus and by train, and frequently wrote from what I saw, overheard, thought. The familiarity of the routes I was taking helped create an intimacy, and writing while traveling seemed to work. Because it was working as a setting I simply used it.

"My poems at the time were becoming more statement oriented, something I was not so accustomed to, and because of this it was often hard for me to tell how my intuition or—at best—intuitions from the poem were functioning. I tried revising this poem a few times, but it seemed to kill the spirit of the piece, and felt as if the revisions were coming from a territory I call 'Should,' which I have learned, slowly, not to trust. My major concern was whether the poem ended with what is the fifth stanza, or with its original (and current) ending.

"The poem is a collage of personal experience, fragments of the experience of friends (one named, one not named), and the overhearing of my own memory.

"I don't recall that there was an actual 'Hotel Tropicana' that I saw. I was more than likely wondering what a 'Hotel Tropicana' would be, and I think this led me to the mood and recollection the poem is."

AMY CLAMPITT was born in New Providence, Iowa, in 1920. She grew up in rural Iowa and attended Grinnell College. She has since lived mainly in New York City. She began publishing poems in magazines in 1978 and has published three full-length collections since 1983: *The Kingfisher* (Knopf, 1983), *What the Light Was Like* (Knopf, 1985) and *Archaic Figure* (Knopf, 1987). She has received a Guggenheim Fellowship (1982) and held appointments as a writer in residence at the College of William and Mary (1984–85) and at Amherst College (1986–87). She is the author of a play, *The Three of Us*, with Dorothy Wordsworth as the central character; a staged reading by the Poets' Theatre in Cambridge, Massachusetts, took place in February 1989.

Of "A Minor Tremor," Clampitt writes: "My one experience of an earthquake was in Berkeley in April 1984. I don't recall trying to write anything about it until more than three years later, as I heard about a severer quake that had occurred in southern California. It appears that I had been rereading Milton around that time; anyhow, I now made a connection between the earthquake I had experienced and the one described in his ode 'On the Morning of Christ's Nativity,' in which the overthrow of all pagan deities and their oracular sites is accompanied by earthquakes, and in which Satan, 'the old Dragon underground, / In straiter limits bound, / Not half so far casts his usurpèd sway, / And, wroth to see his kingdom fail, / Swinges the scaly horror of his folded tail.' And this led in turn to some didactic musings, which I suppose are never very far from my mind, concerning the advanced state of the current decadence."

TOM CLARK was born in Chicago in 1941. He received a B.A. from the University of Michigan and an M.A. from Cambridge University. He has worked variously as a writer, editor, artist, and teacher. His books include many volumes of poetry, several biographies, and two novels. His most recent collection of poems is *Easter Sunday* (Coffee House Press, 1987). From 1963 to 1973 he was *The Paris Review*'s poetry editor. Currently he lives in Berkeley, California.

Clark writes: " 'For Robert Duncan' is a modest little thirty-second elegy for the late great American poet, written within a few days of the news of the death and no doubt principally inspired by the deceased poet's generous conversation in recent years, as well as his last poems, coincidentally just then being published; I suppose if one trained the opera glasses steadily enough, however, one might make out lurking behind the poem's main figure some phantom shade of Orpheus or Osiris, and too the water in the poem might as easily be the Aegean off Lesbos or the Egyptian Nile as San Francisco Bay."

CLARK COOLIDGE was born in Providence, Rhode Island, in 1939. He has lectured at the Naropa Institute in Boulder, Colorado, and at New College of California in San Francisco, and he was a writer-in-residence at the American Academy in Rome (1984–85). Recent books include *Solution Passage (Poems 1978–1981)* (Sun & Moon Press, 1986), *The Crystal Text* (The Figures, 1986), *Mesh* (In Camera, 1988), *At Egypt* (The Figures, 1988), and *Sound as Thought (Poems 1982–1984)* (Sun & Moon Press, forthcoming).

DOUGLAS CRASE was born in Battle Creek, Michigan, in 1944. He is the author of *The Revisionist* (Little, Brown, 1981) and was awarded the Witter Bynner Prize for poetry by the American Academy and Institute of Arts and Letters in 1983. His essays on poetry have appeared in *The Nation*. He has received a Guggenheim Fellowship, a Whiting Writer's Award, and in 1987 a MacArthur Fellowship. He lives in New York City.

Of "True Solar Holiday," Crase writes: "The trouble with talking about a poem is that what you say will repeat or replace or wreck the poem, when the reason you wrote it in the first place was that prose isn't good enough. On continents so clogged with human chat, anybody would think twice about bestowing more waste no landfill will accept. For a time, it was exciting to write and compose and perform in ways said to celebrate randomness, while life, though improbable, seems, even as DNA is, a defense against randomness. The least guileful esthetic may not be exactly upfront, any more than the critic who offers 'this quote I have taken at random.' Whatever it was, it turns out that if you describe it, by poem equation dance performance picture, it is no longer random. Maybe that's why all evolution should end up talking so much."

ROBERT CREELEY was born in Arlington, Massachusetts, in 1926. At Black Mountain College, where he taught between 1954 and 1956, he established and edited *Black Mountain Review*. Since 1966 he has taught at the State University of New York at Buffalo. He spent the 1988–89 academic year as a Fulbright Fellow in Finland. His most recent publications include *The Collected Poems of Robert Creeley, 1945–1975* (University of California Press, 1983), *Collected Essays* (University of California Press, 1989), and his edition of *The Essential Burns* (Ecco Press, 1989). In March 1989 he was made New York State Poet, following Stanley Kunitz in that honor.

Of "Age," Creeley writes: "The poem was written, like they say, as a self-defense of sorts, up in the office I then had at SUNY/Buffalo. To get a parking space I'd come in at eight, although I didn't teach till eleven, and I began to use the spare time for writing. This poem, for example, was broken, in fact, about halfway through by the visit of a welcome student, but went on after he left sans any problem. No doubt the material was fighting for expression. I had had a lousy spring with, first, a fistula, which details of the poem refer to, and next, what I presumed would be mechanical correction of arthritic problems with both big toes, a Silastic Implant Bilateral—which I caution all readers of whatever age to avoid like the veritable plague as well as those who prescribe it. Anyhow, age causes problems obviously, but few the ineptitude of those attending, on either side of that human fence, can't instantly make far worse. Onward!' "

PETER DAVISON was born in New York City in 1928 and was educated at Harvard and Cambridge. He is the author of numerous volumes of poetry, most recently *Praying Wrong: New & Selected Poems 1957–1984* (Atheneum, 1984) and *The Great Ledge* (Knopf, 1989). He is the editor of Peter Davison Books, an imprint of Houghton Mifflin Company, where he also serves as poetry editor. He has in addition been poetry editor of *The Atlantic Monthly* since 1972. He lives in Gloucester and Boston, Massachusetts.

Davison writes: "The first draft of this poem was written on a postcard several years ago to a frequent contributor to *The Atlantic Monthly* by way of conveying more than a 'rejection slip.' What an editor sees in the repeated submissions of poets is more of their lives than they may suspect. I thought I might write, but only as a poem, a sequence of comfortable words to aspirants: yes, I know,

I care, I wish I could tell you so, take heart. This was the outcome: 'A Letter from the Poetry Editor.' "

DAVID DOOLEY was born in Knoxville, Tennessee, in 1947. He received a B.A. in English from Johns Hopkins University and an M.A. in English from the University of Tennessee. His manuscript *The Volcano Inside* won the initial Nicholas Roerich Prize and was published by Story Line Press in 1988. Only one poem from that volume had previously been published in a magazine. He currently lives in San Antonio, Texas, where he works as a legal assistant.

Dooley writes: "How does the world appear to other people? Few questions are more crucial to our moral experience. Dramatic monologues attempt to provide at least partial answers to that question. In 'The Reading' one woman, a psychic, expounds her vision of another woman's life. What subject could be more interesting to a male writer?

"Since the monologue presents a complete play in miniature, many techniques of writing for the theater apply. Imagery must be strictly subordinated to character. An irregularly educated southerner like the psychic in 'The Reading' would not, and must not, sound like a contemporary poet. As anyone who has ever acted, directed, or written for the theater knows, timing is extremely important. Phrases do not all move at the same rate. Like rubato in music, the speech now hesitates, now presses forward. The most effective language for the theater sometimes consists of phrases unremarkable in themselves. The same is true of dramatic monologues. Each element of the poem, like each element of a scene, must contribute to the momentum of the whole. The author of a monologue willingly surrenders the freedoms of imagery and direct comment to explore situations and emotions outside his own experience.

"Like all of my poems, monologues or not, 'The Reading' is intended to be read aloud."

RITA DOVE was born in 1952 and grew up in Akron, Ohio. She graduated from the University of Miami, received a Fulbright Fellowship to study at the University of Tübingen, Germany, and later took an M.F.A. at the University of Iowa. She won the Pulitzer

Prize in poetry for *Thomas and Beulah* (Carnegie-Mellon University Press, 1986). Other poetry books include *The Yellow House on the Corner* (1980) and *Museum* (1983), both from Carnegie-Mellon, and *Grace Notes* (Norton, 1989). She has also published a collection of short stories, *Fifth Sunday*, and is currently working on a novel. She teaches at the University of Virginia in Charlottesville.

Of "The Late Notebooks of Albrecht Dürer," Dove writes: "My obsession with Albrecht Dürer began when I was a student at the Universität Tübingen in West Germany, twenty-two years old and thrilled by every medieval turret and cobblestone. Dürer's engravings seemed to possess the same dark, complicated lines of the buildings and streets in old Tübingen, so I began reading Dürer's letters and diaries as well.

"Poised at the crossroads between the Middle Ages and the Renaissance, Dürer struggled to free himself from the stiff dark composition of medieval German life, which was circumscribed by the social and moral upheavals of his time—the discovery of a New World in 1492, Martin Luther's reformatory approach to the church, and the golden stirrings of the Italian Renaissance. His engravings form a marvelous graph of one soul restlessly redefining itself.

"Only recently have poems begun to emerge from these meditations. 'The Late Notebooks of Albrecht Dürer' is a collage of his meditations and mine—scraps from his treatises, descriptions of engravings, imagined interior monologues. The poem is an attempt to capture the spirit of the running dialogue every artist conducts with him/herself—that peculiar mixture of wonder, rigor, intensity, and desire."

STEPHEN DUNN was born in Forest Hills, New York, in 1939. He is the author of seven collections of poetry, including *Between Angels* (Norton, 1989) and *Local Time*, a National Poetry Series selection. His awards include fellowships from the National Endowment for the Arts and the Guggenheim Foundation, the Levinson Prize from *Poetry*, and the Theodore Roethke and Helen Bullis prizes from *Poetry Northwest*. He is professor of creative writing at Stockton State College in New Jersey.

Of "Letting The Puma Go," Dunn writes: "I remember a few things about the poem's composition. I had seen a PBS special on tigers, and had written in my notebook one fact that had startled me: 'The tiger succeeds only once in twenty hunts.' Some months later I started writing directly about the tiger, but along the way invented a man at a zoo, watching tigers. After a few drafts I had become more interested in the man, his particular loneliness, his timidity. For a while, my working title was 'The Sad Man.' In an early draft I had written the lines that are now the poem's epigraph. At some point they no longer functioned in the poem, but I regretted their loss. Thus the somewhat audacious use of them.

"Many years ago I had written a short poem called 'The Outfielder':

> So this is excellence, movement
> toward the barely possible,
> the puma's dream
> of running down a
> hummingbird
> on a grassy plain.

When I wrote the line 'But he could spend half an afternoon / with those outfielders . . .'" I remembered the poem and found a way to include it. Finally, 'The Sad Man,' a bad title from the beginning, seemed too directive, too limiting, and I gave it up.

"To say that one thing led to another would be both true and false. One thing did lead to another but not always immediately. The reader, of course, should believe otherwise."

RUSSELL EDSON lives in Stamford, Connecticut, with his wife, Frances. His books include, among others, *The Very Thing That Happens* (New Directions, 1964), *What a Man Can See* (The Jargon Society, 1969), *The Childhood of an Equestrian* (Harper & Row, 1973), *The Clam Theater* (Wesleyan University Press, 1973), *The Falling Sickness: Four Plays* (New Directions, 1975), *The Intuitive Journey and Other Works* (Harper & Row, 1976), *The Reason Why the Closet-Man Is Never Sad* (Wesleyan, 1977), *With Sincerest Regrets* (Burning Deck, 1980), *Gulping's Recital*, a novel (Guignol Books, 1984), and *The Wounded Breakfast* (Wesleyan, 1985).

He has received a Guggenheim Fellowship and two National Endowment for the Arts fellowships.

Of "The Rabbit Story," Edson writes: "It would seem the intent here, although this is never completely clear, not even after a piece is written, is to express a certain disquiet we all feel at times about the fate of man. Experience seems random. We come into the world and leave it without our *having to do anything*. We just happen, with or without our volition. Life is always best in its potential. For, *time, the bringer, finally ruins everything*. . . .

"I think, looking at this piece again, I should like the reader to see it as the dance of life, animated as in a short motion picture cartoon."

DANIEL MARK EPSTEIN was born in Washington, D.C., in 1948 and was educated at Kenyon College. He is the author of five books of poetry, including *Young Men's Gold, The Book of Fortune*, and *Spirits*, all published by Overlook/Viking Press. He is also the author of *Star of Wonder* and *Love's Compass*, books of essays. In 1977 he won the Prix de Rome in literature, and in 1982 he was awarded a Guggenheim Fellowship. He lives in Baltimore.

ELAINE EQUI was born in Chicago in 1953 and grew up in Oak Park, Illinois. She is the author of four books of poetry: *Federal Woman* (Danaides Press, 1978), *Shrewcrazy* (Little Caesar Press, 1981), *The Corners of the Mouth* (Iridescence, 1986), and *Accessories* (The Figures, 1988). Two new titles are due out in 1989: *Views Without Rooms* (Hanuman Books) as well as a collection of poems from Coffee House Press. She currently lives in New York City.

Of "A Date with Robbe-Grillet," Equi notes: "Writing a poem in homage to Robbe-Grillet, I wanted to capture some of the echoes and permutations in his work. I found the pantoum to be the most appropriate form to do this. It allowed me to repeat lines in the same way that he repeats scenes, each with a slight variation in context, each stanza containing a memory of the previous one, which it constantly revises."

AARON FOGEL was born in New York City in 1947. His books include *Chain Hearings* (Inwood/Horizon Press, 1976) and *Coercion to Speak* (Harvard University Press, 1985). He has been the recipient of a Kellett Fellowship to study in England (1967–69) and a Guggenheim Fellowship (1987). He teaches at Boston University.

Fogel writes: " 'BW' was written in 1981. The title has no one meaning. It names the field of bw words and phrases. It also comes from *TV Guide*, where the two letters, with a TV-screen-shaped line around them, indicate movies not in color."

ALICE FULTON was born in Troy, New York, in 1952. Her books include *Dance Script with Electric Ballerina* (University of Pennsylvania Press, 1983) and *Palladium* (University of Illinois Press, 1986). She has been a Fellow of the Fine Arts Work Center in Provincetown, the Michigan Society of Fellows, and the Guggenheim Foundation. She teaches at the University of Michigan, Ann Arbor. Her work was included in the 1988 edition of *The Best American Poetry*.

Fulton writes: " 'Powers of Congress' is more regular in form than most of my work. Each line has seven syllables. Five of the seven are accented, making a strong-stress almost sprung-sounding rhythm. Thus language has been subjected to considerable pressure in the making of this poem. Meaning resists such distillation, and this resistance gives the lines a bursting, combustible quality. The poem's form acts as a kind of spark screen to a scarcely contained fire; it shields the reader from the chaos of unformed utterance while allowing glimpses of the flammable energy contained. One of the poem's concerns is union: the unthinking meshes of nature and the lawful forging of lives in wedlock. Couplings can involve a violent chemistry, as when trees and fire meet to form ashes in a stove. On the other hand, some unions, like the marriages sketched in the last few lines, are the products of stasis. Most broadly, then, this is a poem about change and resistance to change. I hoped the muscular language would underscore the imagery of molten steel cast into solid stoves and trees transformed to heat. (Woodburning stoves often have names like *Defiant* or *Intrepid*. The one in the poem is called *Resolute*, playing upon the wish for stability and fear of flux.) The tightly constructed lines are meant to convey the energy released or contained when objects or people are enmeshed in mutual sway; the poem describes the emotional and physical outcomes of such powerful congress."

SUZANNE GARDINIER was born in New Bedford in 1961 and grew up in Scituate, Massachusetts. She graduated from the University of Massachusetts in 1981 and from the Columbia University M.F.A. program in 1986. She has had poems published in *Grand Street, The New Yorker, The Paris Review*, and other journals; her work also appears in *Under 35: The New Generation of American Poets* (Doubleday, 1989). She teaches, works as assistant editor at *Grand Street*, and is writing a book-length poem called "The New World."

Gardinier writes: " 'Voyage' was written in the summer of 1987, when I was falling in love. When I started it, in New York, I kept the folded sheets in my pockets and sang the tune of it to myself on the West Side IRT and in the burrito place in Sheridan Square; the rhymes would come to me while I was walking or reading tree books or trying to sleep on the hot nights. I finished the last line in a back room of a house in Vermont, while the woman I'd fallen in love with cooked supper and laughed with friends in the kitchen. All summer I had to do without the ocean, and without what felt like almost everything I needed to love someone well for a long time. The poem gave me some of both of those things."

DEBORA GREGER was born in 1949. She received her B.A. at the University of Washington and her M.F.A. at the University of Iowa. Two collections of her poems have been published by Princeton University Press: *Movable Islands* (1980) and *And* (1986). She has received grants from the National Endowment for the Arts (1978 and 1985), the Guggenheim Foundation (1987), and the Ingram Merrill Foundation (1981). She has also been awarded an Amy Lowell Traveling Poetry Scholarship (1981) and a Peter I. B. Lavan Younger Poets Award from the Academy of American Poets (1987). She teaches in the creative writing program of the University of Florida at Gainesville.

LINDA GREGG was born in Suffern, New York, in 1942. She received her B.A. and M.A. degrees at San Francisco State University. She is the author of *Too Bright to See* (Graywolf Press, 1981) and *Alma* (Random House, 1985). She has received a Guggenheim Fellowship and a Whiting Writer's Award. She lives in Northampton, Massachusetts.

Of "A Dark Thing Inside the Day," Gregg writes: "This poem was written while I was living on the Greek island of Lesbos. It's about the light rather than the dark. It's a poem about the light as well as the dark, it is about happiness while acknowledging the serious difficulties of the heart. It's part of my recently completed third volume, *Whoever We May Finally Be*."

THOM GUNN was born in Gravesend, England, in 1929. He was educated at Trinity College, Cambridge University, and did graduate work at Stanford. He has published nine books of poetry, of which the following are in print: *Moly* and *My Sad Captains* (in one volume, 1971), *Jack Straw's Castle* (1976), *Selected Poems* (1979), and *The Passages of Joy* (1982), all published by Farrar, Straus, and Giroux. His book of essays, *The Occasions of Poetry*, was published in 1982 by Faber and Faber in London. He lives in San Francisco.

Of "Cafeteria in Boston," Gunn writes: "People love talking about how they wrote poems; it is so much easier than writing new ones. I am no exception.

"The cafeteria in this poem actually had another name, but it was also the name of someone I had been in love with, so I changed it, as I didn't want to confuse my associations.

"The poem is about what I really ate and what really happened, but to start with there was other stuff in it, things I had on my mind, but I realized (as so often) in revising and rewriting what I truly wanted to write about, so I cut out what I had originally emphasized, and what had started as a couple of details became the poem I ended up with.

"The first friend I showed it to said that the poem just gave him a stomach ache, so I almost didn't print it. I still don't know if it is any good or not. It is one of those poems where I don't clearly see what I have done."

DONALD HALL, the guest editor of *The Best American Poetry, 1989*, was born in New Haven, Connecticut, in 1928. He graduated from Harvard in 1951, studied at Oxford, and taught English at the University of Michigan from 1957 until 1975. Since then he has been a free-lance writer. In 1988 he published *The One Day* (Ticknor & Fields), which won the National Book Critics Circle Award in poetry. In the same year he gathered his fourth collection of essays about poetry, *Poetry and Ambition* (University of Michigan Press). Other recent books include *The Happy Man*, poems (Random House, 1986), and *The Ideal Bakery*, short stories (North Point Press, 1987).

Hall writes: " 'History' is one of 'Four Classic Texts' in *The One Day*. Each text exaggerates concerns prevalent elsewhere in the poem, and alludes by pastiche and parody to old models. 'History' looks back to the prose of Thucydides, Tacitus, Caesar, Gibbon, and the minor historians who are Gibbon's sources. The method is anachronism, which I learned from Gibbon. When you read Gibbon you read two books at once. One is about the decline and fall of the Roman Empire; the other embodies the Enlightenment. Of course Shakespeare's midsummer Thebans are Englishmen, and anachronism is always with us. The deliberate conflation of eras, as when John Ball conspires with Spartacus, makes a familiar modernist trope. Many stories in 'History' are true to their references, like Livy's account of Titus Manlius, and many derive not from the old world but from the Boston *Globe*. Other figures are invented, like Senex, or generic, like 'the prime minister.' (The third stanza is paraphrased from a letter by Richard Courant.) Parallels suggest universals: When I alluded to the color gangs of Byzantium, I was not aware of the color gangs of Los Angeles."

JOHN HOLLANDER was born in New York City in 1929. Among his recent books are *Powers of Thirteen* (Atheneum, 1983) and *Harp Lake* (Knopf, 1988) as well as two theoretical studies, *Melodious Guile* (Yale University Press, 1988) and *The Figure of Echo* (University of California Press, 1981). A new and enlarged edition of his *Rhyme's Reason: A Guide to English Verse* is scheduled for publication in fall 1989 by Yale University Press. In 1988 he was nominated for National Book Critics Circle awards in both poetry and criticism. He is A. Bartlett Giamatti Professor of English at Yale.

Of "Kinneret," Hollander writes that the title derives from "*Yam Kinneret*, the Sea of Galilee, whose name may be related to the word *kinnor*, or *harp*." He adds: "The disjunct form of these quatrains is borrowed from the Malay *pantun* (not from its fussy, refrain-plagued

French derivative, the *pantoum*), in which the first and second lines frame one sentence, and the next two another, apparently unrelated one. These two are superficially connected only by the cross-rhyming in the quatrain and by some common construction, scheme, pun, assonance, or the like. But below the surface, they are united in some deeper parable. A self-descriptive example of the form shows this most clearly:

Catamaran

Pantuns in the original Malay
　　Are quatrains of two thoughts, but of one mind,
Athwart my two pontoons I sail away,
　　Yet touching neither; land lies far behind.

The expository disjuncture in these stanzas extends even to the personages referred to by pronouns, and 'he' or 'she' are quite different in the first and last two lines. But the groups of four quatrains are rhythmically paced: there is a refrainlike return, in every fourth stanza, of some allusion to the lake over whose tranquillity and beauty, remembered from early spring evenings, I was brooding over during the rather personally agitated weeks during which this poem was composed.''

PAUL HOOVER was born in Harrisonburg, Virginia, in 1946. He is the author of four books of poetry, including *Idea* (The Figures, 1987), winner of the Carl Sandburg Award for poetry, and *Nervous Songs* (L'Epervier Press, 1986). He has received a General Electric Award for Younger Writers and a National Endowment for the Arts poetry fellowship. His first novel, *Saigon, Illinois*, was published by Vintage Contemporaries in 1988. Together with his wife, the writer Maxine Chernoff, he edits the Chicago-based magazine *New American Writing*.

　Hoover writes: " 'The Novel' is a sixty-page poem written in reaction to having written a novel in six months that was immediately accepted for publication. The forces behind the poem are astonishment and disappointment, resulting in an examination of authorship, especially that of the novelist, at once the commonest and most lordly of authors. Why are certain forms of literature privileged over others? In 'The Novel' poetry's frustrations and fiction's privilege dance cheek to cheek. In section twenty-five it is perhaps poetry that prepares a 'nor' for the 'never' we'd extended. Self-canceling ironies part like curtains, leaving the poem nude on the page: 'Poetry is important fiction, / thought the dead Marine.' As in the rest of the long poem, narratives intervene, especially inelegant apparitions from genre novels. Section twenty-five begins with the white bear of *Tristram Shandy* as object of perception, main character, and image of the baggy-pantsed author throwing his weight around ('shaking like meat, insolvent as water'). Several foolish authorial postures follow, allowing for the beating of significant wings (lacking Leda, poetry dizzies itself with its own wingbeats). Self-consciousness is opaque; the world is transparent. The middle part of the section offers a parody of Vietnam fiction (Lieutenant Gorge). The ending appeals to experience (death). The reader, almost as space traveler, enters a grainy photograph and is swallowed by nebulous astral dots. The grain of being and the grainy photograph offer a palimpsest: art and being enter each other like mirror and water."

MARIE HOWE was born in Rochester, New York, in 1950. She received her B.A. at the University of Windsor, Ontario, in 1972, and her M.F.A. at Columbia University in 1983. She is the author of *The Good Thief* (Persea Books, 1987). A recent recipient of the Peter I. B. Lavan Younger Poets Award from the Academy of American Poets, she lives in Cambridge, Massachusetts, and teaches at Tufts University.

Of "The Good Reason for Our Forgetting," Howe writes: "One summer night several years ago in Vermont, I came home to the little carriage house I was living in to find it inexplicably dark and empty. My brother should have been there with a friend who was visiting. Their cigarettes were still on the table, a jacket on the back of a chair. And I was suddenly seized with the conviction that they, along with the members of the larger house, had been devoured by a beast I could still sense in the area, very near. I thought I heard it outside the bathroom window chewing on something. I stood still a long time wondering what to do and where to go before I heard steps on the outside stairs and a knock on the glass door. It was my brother and his friend, returning from dinner. They calmed me down, we all laughed, and in the subsequent conversation my brother told me one of the stories embedded in the poem, a true story about a six-year-old boy who was left alone with his father for three days when his mother went on a holiday with her sister. The father died on the first day. My brother had heard the story from the man the boy had grown up into. When the odd chewing sound started up again we all walked to the window to see a white pony calmly eating grass in the moonlight. Nevertheless, the next day, the cat disappeared and never came back."

ANDREW HUDGINS was born in Killeen, Texas, in 1951 and grew up in Montgomery, Alabama. He was educated at Huntingdon College and at Alabama, Syracuse, Iowa, and Stanford universities. Currently he teaches at the University of Cincinnati. During the 1989–90 academic year he will be the Alfred Hodder Fellow at Princeton University. He has published two books of poetry: *Saints and Strangers* (Houghton Mifflin, 1985) and *After the Lost War: A Narrative* (Houghton Mifflin, 1988).

Of "Heat Lightning in a Time of Drought," Hudgins writes: "One of the things I like about this poem is that it allowed me to tell a joke that I think is the most psychologically astute joke I have ever heard."

RODNEY JONES's books of poetry are *The Story They Told Us of Light* (University of Alabama Press, 1980), *The Unborn* (Atlantic Monthly Press, 1985), and *Transparent Gestures* (Houghton Mifflin, 1989). Born in Falkville, Alabama, in 1950, he attended the universities of Alabama and North Carolina at Greensboro. His awards include fellowships from the National Endowment for the Arts and the Guggenheim Foundation, a General Electric Award, and the Peter I. B. Lavan Younger Poets Award from the Academy of American Poets. Jones lives with his wife and daughter in Carbondale, Illinois, where he teaches English at Southern Illinois University.

Of "Every Day There Are New Memos," Jones writes: "I work for a state, so I receive many concentrated and sterilized conversations. My full mailbox is a function of demographics, of paranoia, of the archive that must be opened should litigation, like an Old Testament plague, ever descend on the institution. And yet I clearly prefer language that characterizes a speaker or writer to language that pretends objective representation. The names that most corporations agree to answer to are as inhuman as the architecture of their executive office buildings. But this poem is a laboriously accomplished moral fantasy: both memos and graffiti are rather shy ways to mark territory that is, after all, academic. We actualized humans make poems, and this one was improved considerably by changes recommended by Stephen Corey and Stan Lindberg."

LAWRENCE JOSEPH was born in Detroit, Michigan, in 1948. He was educated at the University of Michigan, where he won the Hopwood Award for poetry; Cambridge University, where he read English literature; and the University of Michigan Law School. His first book of poems, *Shouting at No One*, received the 1982 Starrett Poetry Prize and was published by the University of Pittsburgh Press in 1983. His second collection, *Curriculum Vitae*—which includes "An Awful Lot Was Happening"—appeared in the Pitt Poetry Series in 1988. Among his awards is a National Endowment for the Arts poetry fellowship. He is presently professor of law at St. John's University School of Law and lives in New York City.

DONALD JUSTICE was born in Miami, Florida, in 1925. His first book, *The Summer Anniversaries* (Wesleyan University Press, 1960), was the Lamont Poetry Selection for 1959. It was followed by *Night Light* (Wesleyan, 1967), *Departures* (Atheneum, 1973), and *Selected Poems* (Atheneum, 1979), which was awarded the Pulitzer Prize in 1980. He has also edited *The Collected Poems of Weldon Kees* (University of Nebraska Press, 1962). His latest book is *The Sunset Maker* (Atheneum, 1988). He teaches at the University of Florida.

Justice writes: " 'Dance Lessons of the Thirties' is the last of a series of poems about early music teachers I had."

VICKIE KARP was born in New York City. Her poetry has most recently appeared in *The New York Review of Books*, *The New Yorker*, and *Under 35: The New Generation of American Poets*. She is currently completing a first collection of poems entitled *Police Sift New Clues in Search for Beauty*. In 1988, her documentary film, *Marianne Moore: In Her Own Image*, ran as part of the "Voices and Visions" series on PBS, and her play, *Driving to the Interior*, was staged at the Symphony Space Theatre in New York and the Annenberg Theatre in Philadelphia. She is on the staff of *The New Yorker*.

Of "Getting Dressed in the Dark," Karp writes: "There is something physically poetic, I think, about those moments between sleeping and waking we experience daily. For several minutes, our emotions pay equal respect to the images of our unconscious and the images of consciousness. It is, to put it romantically, the hour of the poet in each of us, and so I thought it might be fun to play with it in a poem. I have, I hope, turned the plain routine of getting dressed into a metaphor for arming oneself with full consciousness and allowed the mundane word *dark* to stand for all sorts of darknesses."

JANE KENYON was born in Ann Arbor, Michigan, in 1947. She attended the University of Michigan. Her books of poetry are *From Room to Room* (Alice James Books, 1978) and *The Boat of Quiet Hours* (Graywolf Press, 1986). She translated *Twenty Poems of Anna Akhmatova* (Eighties/Ally Press, 1985). She lives in New Hampshire.

Of "Three Songs at the End of Summer," Kenyon writes: "This poem is personal, and painful, and it is the kind of poetry I'd like to turn away from. There's very little invention in it. It is memory and reportage."

KENNETH KOCH was born in Cincinnati, Ohio, in 1925. He graduated from Harvard in 1948 and took a doctorate at Columbia University eleven years later. His books of poetry include *Thank You* (Grove, 1962), *When the Sun Tries to Go On* (Black Sparrow, 1969), *The Pleasures of Peace* (Grove, 1969), *The Art of Love* (Random House, 1975), *Days and Nights* (Random House, 1982), and *On the Edge* (Viking, 1986). He is the author of four books on education, including *Wishes, Lies and Dreams* (Vintage, 1971) and *Rose, Where Did You Get That Red?* (Random House, 1973). Koch's *Selected Poems, 1950–1982* was published in 1985 by Random House. *One*

Thousand Avant-Garde Plays (Knopf) appeared in 1988. He is a professor of English at Columbia University and lives in New York City.

Of "Six *Hamlets*," Koch writes: " '*Smoking Hamlet*' was the first of these *Hamlet* variations I thought of. I was in Paris in 1955 and thinking, I don't remember why, about the theater. I was interested in how the play would be changed simply by Hamlet's smoking cigarettes. I remember talking about the idea with my wife, Janice, and Stanley Kunitz—and, as I recall, we came up with another version (not included in my book), *Hamlet on Roller Skates*. The rest of these six *Hamlets* were written later (in 1987 and '88). I am particularly interested in the dramatic possibilities of a full-scale production of the entire play in the style of *Hamlet Rebus*—a version, that is, in which all the imagery, all the figurative language of the play, would be acted out or otherwise physically present on stage. This would to some degree correspond to what the play is like for me (and I would guess for others too) to read, and could be, I think, wonderfully dramatic."

PHILLIS LEVIN was born in Paterson, New Jersey, in 1954. A graduate of Sarah Lawrence (1976) and the Johns Hopkins University Writing Seminars (1977), she has received an Ingram Merrill Foundation fellowship and is an editor of *Boulevard*. She teaches in the M.F.A. program of the University of Maryland at College Park.

Levin writes: "I wrote 'The Ransom' on Easter Sunday 1985. Though the poem went through numerous subsequent revisions, the plot, down to the words in quotation, recounts a dream I had the night before, from which I woke with the disturbing knowledge that I had lost—for reasons beyond my control or grasp—the chance to save another person's life. The title of the poem, and with typical dream logic the whole content, was suggested by my reading John Crowe Ransom before going to sleep; and Ransom's name and work clearly contribute to the absurd, ironic timbre of the experience. When I wrote the piece, I was not reflecting on the crucifixion, the meaning of Christ's sacrifice, or even the fact of having such a dream the night before Easter; my concern was putting into language that unresolved, uncanny experience, keeping it alive through the testament of the poem. Only in retrospect do I see that the dream is in many ways an allegory of the dilemma of the modern artist filled with the heroic impulses of the past but unable to fulfill them on a contemporary stage."

PHILIP LEVINE was born in Detroit, Michigan, in 1928. *On the Edge*, his first book of poems, was published in 1953 by Stone Wall Press. The title poem of his most recent collection, *A Walk with Tom Jefferson* (Knopf, 1988), appeared in last year's edition of *The Best American Poetry*. Levine has won the National Book Critics Circle Award, the American Book Award, the Lenore Marshall Award, and an Award of Merit from the National Institute of Arts and Letters. He has lived in Fresno, California, on and off since 1958.

Levine writes: "The first draft for 'Dog Poem' was written in the late seventies, but I was never happy with the ending so never tried to publish it or read it publicly. In the summer of '86 I happened across it and wrote a new ending in an hour. I don't actually dislike all dogs—I've even loved a few—but I hated them as a kid and later as a delivery man for Railway Express and still later as a mailman. I wanted to write a poem that would be as far from Rilke as I could possibly get and yet could manage to incorporate one moment of that Rilkean grandeur that broods in so much recent American poetry, hence my satisfaction with the new conclusion of the poem. I want to apologize to Louisa Solano, my dear friend and owner of the Grolier Bookstore, for any pain this poem has caused her. I know that Pumpkin is a creature of great sensitivity and intelligence, and this poem was never intended to betray his affections."

ANNE MacNAUGHTON was born in Little Rock, Arkansas, in 1945. She was educated at Colorado College, the University of Texas, and the University of Michigan, and she has worked as an archivist of historical papers for the state of Texas. She currently teaches history in Taos, New Mexico, and works with Taos Pueblo youth. She is co-founder of the Taos Poetry Circus, which stages the World Heavyweight Championship Poetry Bout every summer. Each contestant reads ten poems, and an audience panel renders the verdict. In 1989 defending champion Victor Hernandez Cruz took on challenger Anne Waldman.

Of "Teste Moanial," MacNaughton writes: "The poem was written as a performance piece for The Luminous Animal, a jazz-poetry ensemble in Taos. I always do it to a jazz accompaniment. It was previously published as 'Balls.' "

HARRY MATHEWS was born in New York City in 1930. His most recent books are *Armenian Papers: Poems 1954–1984* (Princeton University Press, 1987), *20 Lines a Day* (Dalkey Archive Press, 1988), and *Cigarettes*, his fourth novel (Collier Books, 1988). His first two novels, *The Conversions* (1962) and *Tlooth* (1966), were recently reissued in paperback by Carcanet Press. He has lived for long periods in France and currently divides his time between Paris and New York.

ROBERT MAZZOCCO was born in 1932 in New York City, where he still lives. His poetry collection, *Trader*, was published in 1980 by Knopf. He is a longtime contributor to *The New York Review of Books* and *The New Yorker*.

Mazzocco writes: "Essentially 'Kidnapped' is a dream poem. A poem about mortality, about youth and age. The shifting details, the drifting imagery, (nautical, theological, medical), as well as the hallucinatory atmosphere, all emphasize, I hope, that point. While the sorrowing boy, the 'runaway child,' carrying his copy of *Kidnapped*, is a kind of David Balfour in negative. In the Stevenson novel, David Balfour, the orphan, is shanghaied and sent to sea, where he undergoes hardship and danger and ultimately learns the lesson about strength through adversity. The boy in the poem does not. Or will not. And hovering above the poem is perhaps the presence of Stevenson himself—the ailing adventurer traveling halfway around the world to die thousands of miles from England on a little island in the South Pacific. When I was in Samoa I made the long corkscrewing trek up to the peak of Mount Vaea to visit Stevenson's grave. Unlike 'Vailima,' Stevenson's home, down below, still on official display, Stevenson's white Arthurian tombstone was not in unkempt splendor. It had been allowed to run to seed, the famous inscription ('Home is the sailor . . .') barely legible. It was a remote and wild place, unknown, for the most part, to even the people of the island. I like to think of the discrepancy here—sad and ironic—as yet another comment on mortality and embedded somewhere in the poem."

JAMES McCORKLE was born in St. Petersburg, Florida, in 1954. He lives in upstate New York, where he has been teaching at Hobart and William Smith Colleges. He is the author of *The Still Performance* (University of Virginia Press, 1989), on recent American poetry, and the editor of *Conversant Essays: Poets on Poetics* (Wayne State University Press, 1989). His poems have appeared in such journals as *The Antioch Review, Boulevard, Denver Quarterly, Missouri Review*, and *The Southwest Review*.

Of "Showing Us the Fields," McCorkle writes: "The poem is set in rural New Jersey. In no particular order, the varied internal rhythms of the long line, an interest in astronomy, and reflections on solitude and various forms of transgression informed the poem. The stories of place, what is rooted in a particular site, have always been important to me."

ROBERT McDOWELL was born in Alhambra, California, in 1953. His first book, *Quiet Money*, was published by Henry Holt in 1987. His criticism, fiction, and poetry appear in such periodicals as *The American Scholar, The Hudson Review, London Magazine*, and *Poets & Writers*. With the poet and critic Mark Jarman he co-edits *The Reaper*, a magazine devoted to the resurgence of narrative in contemporary poetry. Since 1985, he has been the publisher of Story Line Press. Under that imprint, he has edited an anthology of essays, *Poetry After Modernism*, which will be published in September 1989. He lives in Santa Cruz, California.

McDowell writes: 'The Fifties' is the first chapter (of five) of *Home in America*, a book-length poem in blank verse. The narrative follows the fortunes, both good and ill, of one American family through the last five decades of the twentieth century. In the poem, I have attempted to build on the sudden shifts of psychological perspective one finds in a poet like Robinson Jeffers, making them quicker and more cinematic. All good narrative begins with characters who take hold of us and won't let go. In them, we must recognize what is familiar in ourselves; we must also admit the surprises that amuse or disturb us. The pentameter line, for me, provides a more muscular vehicle for sustaining a coherent poem of length, adapting itself to the full range of lyric, meditative, and storytelling possibilities in our language."

WESLEY McNAIR was born in Newport, New Hampshire, in 1941. His two books of verse are *The Faces of Americans in 1853* (University of Missouri Press Breakthrough Series, 1984), which won the Devins Award in 1984, and *The Town of No*, published by David R. Godine in 1989. He has received a Guggenheim Fellowship in poetry, two fellowship grants from the National Endowment for the Arts (one of them for 1989–90), the Pushcart Prize, and the Eunice Tietjens Memorial Prize from *Poetry*. His poetry has appeared in *The Atlantic Monthly, Poetry, Harvard Magazine, Yankee, The Iowa Review, The Kenyon Review*, and *Ploughshares*. He is currently a professor of creative writing at the Farmington campus of the University of Maine.

Of "The Abandonment," McNair writes: "When I wrote this poem, a few months after my brother's death, it felt like a scream—the voice of my fear and rage and grief, barely controlled by language. To my surprise, a friend who read it told me the poem's voice seemed distant and detached. I saw then that my poem was far more objective than I had realized—that its long sentence was a way of glimpsing all at once actions I had never seen, and storing them away."

JAMES MERRILL was born in New York City in 1926. He received his B.A. from Amherst College in 1947 and published his *First Poems* in 1951 (Knopf). His books have received two National Book Awards, the Pulitzer Prize, and the Bollingen Prize in poetry. The epic poem begun in *Divine Comedies* (Atheneum, 1976) and extended in two subsequent volumes was published in its entirety as *The Changing Light at Sandover* (Atheneum, 1983), which won the National Books Critics Circle Award. His most recent books are *Late Settings* (Atheneum, 1985) and *The Inner Room* (Knopf, 1988). He divides his time between Stonington, Connecticut, and Key West, Florida.

*   *   *

THYLIAS MOSS was born in Cleveland, Ohio, in 1954. She teaches English at Phillips Academy in Andover, Massachusetts. Her second collection of poems, *Pyramid of Bone*, was published by Callaloo/University of Virginia Press in 1989. She received a National Endowment for the Arts poetry fellowship for 1989.

Moss writes: " 'The Warmth of Hot Chocolate' is a poem of my reconciliation with God, not the God of my Baptist upbringing, the one keeping tally of my soul's absolute devotion to Him and no other by watching my every move, including the elimination of my bodily wastes; no, not that voyeur God I met in Sunday school before old enough to start kindergarten, not the one who created weak flesh then condemned, *damned* for that very weakness; not him. What made sense to me as a child; what still makes sense is that simple, sometimes trite, even exploited definition of God as love. What makes sense to me is that a God made of love would be subject to all of love's fickleness, all of its blindnesses and inconsistencies as well as its pleasures and powers of cure. He would have to fall just as we do to access love.

"How simple then to go the next step of literal interpretation of being made in his image—not just me, but everyone. All of us the result of God assigning to each of us a small part of him. The never-ending work of that assigning, for he is so large, he needs billions of us before all parts of him may be represented.

"Through the poem, I send to God my gratefulness. I can think of no one who would willingly take his job of absolute responsibility. I can think of his hurt as he is rejected, outgrown. I can think of two ways to terminate him: a universe of believers, literally heaven, utopia, when heaven and hell both lose definition in the absence of contrast; and a totality of nonbelievers leading of course to the same loss of definition for the same reason. Though I'm seldom sure why—one part pity perhaps?—I must do what I can to see that neither course of termination is followed to completion. Because the totality of nonbelievers seems less likely to me, the poem offers the perspective of one committed to preserving a need for God's continued existence. An angel because such an act of commitment could come from only one whose love of and devotion to God were large enough. From one whose dependence on him was absolute. Someone close enough to him to understand him.

Someone much as a spouse would be if spouses could be closer than currently possible."

SHARON OLDS was born in San Francisco in 1942 and educated at Stanford and Columbia universities. She has published three books of poetry: *Satan Says* (University of Pittsburgh Press, 1980; San Francisco Poetry Center Award), *The Dead and the Living* (Knopf, 1984; Lamont Selection of the Academy of American Poets; National Book Critics Circle Award), and *The Gold Cell* (Knopf, 1987). She is completing a collection called *The Father*. She is director of creative writing at New York University; she teaches writing workshops there and at Goldwater Hospital (for the physically disabled), Roosevelt Island, New York.

Old writes: " 'The Wellspring' was written in Pennsylvania—in a lot of Pennsylvania. It came to me on a train from Pittsburgh to New York City. The first nine-tenths of it was written before we were much out of Pittsburgh. Then it took eight hours to find the ending, or for the ending to find me. I wrote and wrote, and crossed out and crossed out. It's something that happens to me sometimes —getting stuck on an ending for hours and hours. Probably lots of people would leave it then—take a break—and that's probably the right thing to do. I just can't. The poem keeps pulling at me. It pulls me back to the point where it starts to go wrong. It won't let me go ('I will not let thee go, except thou bless me'). I have to finish it, according to its own lights, before I can be free of it and it of me: that moment, after you blow the bubble, when you close your lips, and the bubble floats off, separate, complete. But first I have to find that ending. Or the train has to get me to it! This ending was waiting for me almost at home. When I saw, across the reed swamps and the Palisades, the tiny steeples of Manhattan, I 'got' it. And I saw how it had to stand on a narrow base, slightly wobbly—to be balanced, over the thin ground of its last line, on a rather round heel."

MARY OLIVER lives in Provincetown, Massachusetts. Her books include *Twelve Moons* (Little, Brown, 1979); *American Primitive* (Atlantic/Little, Brown, 1983); and *Dream Work* (Atlantic Monthly Press, 1986). She received the Pulitzer Prize in 1984 for *American Primitive*.

STEVE ORLEN was born in Holyoke, Massachusetts, in 1942. His most recent book of poems is *A Place at the Table* (Holt, Rinehart, and Winston, 1982). He is the director of the creative writing program at the University of Arizona. "The Bridge of Sighs" is the title poem of a new manuscript.

MICHAEL PALMER was born in New York City in 1943. He has lived in San Francisco since 1969. His two most recent collections are *First Figure* (1984) and *Sun* (1988), both from North Point Press. He is currently a visiting lecturer at the University of California at San Diego. The poem "Sun" appeared not only in Palmer's book of that title but also in *O One*, an anthology edited by Leslie Scalapino and published by O Press (1988).

Palmer writes: " 'Sun' came as both echo and alternative to my much longer poem of the same title. It was generated in part by a headline in the Boston *Globe*, 'Neak Luong Is a Blur.' The article discussed American combatants' fading memories of the war in Cambodia."

BOB PERELMAN was born in Youngstown, Ohio, in 1947. His books of poems include *The First World* (The Figures, 1986), *Face Value* (Roof Press, 1988), and *Captive Audience* (The Figures, 1988). He is the editor of *Writing/Talks* (1985), an anthology of talks by writers, published by Southern Illinois University Press. His work appeared in last year's edition of *The Best American Poetry*. He lives in Berkeley, California, with his wife and two children.

ROBERT PINSKY was born in Long Branch, New Jersey, in 1940. He has published three books of poetry: *Sadness and Happiness* (1975) and *An Explanation of America* (1979), both from Princeton University Press, and *History of My Heart* (Ecco, 1984). He is also the author of an interactive computer novel, *Mindwheel* (Broderbund, 1985). His book of essays, *Poetry and the World* (Ecco, 1988), was nominated for the National Book Critics Circle Award in criticism. In spring 1990, Ecco will publish his new book of poems, *The Want Bone*. "At Pleasure Bay" will be the final poem in the collection.

Pinsky writes: "Pleasure Bay is a real place, part of my hometown of Long Branch, New Jersey, where the Shrewsbury River meets the Atlantic Ocean. Near the inlet there once was a swing bridge as described in the poem, and Price's Hotel and Theater, where in the summer parties from New York came by boat to have dinner, see the show, and spend the night in a romantic setting among cool shore breezes. All gone now, for a housing tract and shopping center. The theater burned down before I was born, but I can remember watching the swing bridge when I was a child. My father has often pointed out to me the place where the chief of police and his lover committed suicide in a car."

ANNA RABINOWITZ was born in Brooklyn, New York. She has been a teacher in the New York City schools, an editor, an interior designer, and a professor at the Fashion Institute of Technology in New York City. Her work has appeared in *Sulfur, Wind*, and *Poetry Northwest*. At present she is completing her thesis for an M.F.A. in writing at Columbia University. She has three grown children and lives with her husband in Manhattan.

Of "Sappho Comments on an Exhibition of Expressionist Land-scapes," Rabinowitz writes: "This poem emerged as the result of a conversation my daughter and I had after viewing an exhibition of Expressionist landscapes at the IBM Gallery in New York. Susan was then completing her degree in fine arts at the University of Michigan and she was having some concerns about her painting. Much of our discussion revolved around art made by males vs. art made by females, and at one point Susan flippantly said something about women needing penises. I couldn't get her remark out of my mind. I also had been wanting to try my hand at Sapphics. I can't remember quite how it happened, but in one of those Daemon-orchestrated moments we experience, Sappho herself came forth as the spokeswoman and put it all together."

MARK RUDMAN was born in New York City in 1948. At present he lives there and teaches in the writing program of New York University. His books include *By Contraries: Poems 1970–84* (National Poetry Foundation, 1987) and *Robert Lowell: An Introduction to the Poetry* (Columbia University Press, 1983). He has translated Boris

Pasternak's *My Sister—Life, and The Sublime Malady* (Ardis Press, 1983; rev. ed., 1989). He is the editor of *Pequod*.

Rudman writes: " 'The Shoebox' came to me when I was at a chamber music concert in a small recital hall in Maine listening to a Fauré quartet. It was late July and sweltering. Amidst the racket of crickets and cicadas, the music seemed to take hold of the air, rise and fade. As the musicians, dripping sweat, drew their bows across the strings of violin and cello, I imagined they were drawing sound out of the instruments, and the tension of their performance in the heat, the screeching and slipping of bow on string, gave birth to the image of the 'rubber bands / wound taut as bowstrings around the top'—a fragile balance. I didn't see how matter could hold together in the heat, how it could keep on stretching itself—living! The stops and starts of the poem probably correspond to the pattern of the music, each sound, each image, demanding attention, then demanding to be passed over, circumvented, to make way for the next, lest the past threaten to swallow the present. Scribbling maniacally over the program notes, the first of some fifty drafts, I didn't think about the content of the poem, only how to get the box open and shut again, knowing that all such attempts are provisional. We are never 'done' with anything in psychic life. But I would make music out of this useless, ominous box."

DAVID ST. JOHN was born in California in 1949. He is the author of three collections of poetry: *Hush* (1976), *The Shore* (1980), and *No Heaven* (1985), all from Houghton-Mifflin. A recipient of fellowships from the National Endowment for the Arts, the Guggenheim Foundation, and the Ingram Merrill Foundation, he is poetry editor of *The Antioch Review* and a professor of English at the University of Southern California.

St. John writes: "The dramatic monologue 'Broken Gauges' is an homage to my two favorite writers of the American West, Sam Shepard and Larry Levis."

YVONNE SAPIA was born in New York City in 1946. She has published two collections of poetry: *The Fertile Crescent* (Anhinga Press, 1983) and *Valentino's Hair* (Northeastern University Press, 1987), which won the Morse Poetry Prize. Her awards include a fellowship from the National Endowment for the Arts and two fellowships from the Florida Arts Council. She has spent most of her life in Florida, where she teaches and serves as series editor for the yearly Anhinga Prize in Poetry. At present she is completing her doctoral studies at Florida State University in Tallahassee and lives in Lake City.

Of "Valentino's Hair," Sapia writes: "By the time I was old enough to recognize misfortune, my father, Facundo the barber, was a poor old man who had little to leave his daughter. But he gave me an inheritance in the story he shared with me about the day he cut Rudolph Valentino's hair. My imagination took over from that point. And writing this poem encouraged a new voice, a narrative voice, perhaps that lost voice missing from much contemporary poetry, a voice I like, a voice I am still exploring."

LYNDA SCHRAUFNAGEL was born in Ashland, Wisconsin, in 1950. She received her B.A. from the University of Washington and her M.A. from the University of Houston. Her poems have appeared in *Feminist Studies* and *Shenandoah*, among other periodicals. She lives in Seattle, Washington, where she works as a teacher and editor.

DAVID SHAPIRO was born in Newark, New Jersey, in 1947. A violinist in his youth, he graduated from Columbia University in 1968 and then studied at Clare College, Cambridge, on a Kellett Fellowship. His books of poetry include *January* (Holt, Rinehart, and Winston, 1965); *A Man Holding an Acoustic Panel* (Dutton, 1971), which was nominated for a National Book Award; *The Page-Turner* (Liveright, 1973); *To an Idea* (Overlook Press, 1983); and *House (Blown Apart)* (Overlook, 1988). He has published a critical study of John Ashbery's poetry as well as monographs on the painters Jim Dine and Jasper Johns. Currently an associate professor of art history at William Paterson College in Wayne, New Jersey, he lives in New York with his wife and son.

Shapiro writes: " 'The Lost Golf Ball' was inspired by the poetry of 'romantic' physics. An article in the *Times* announced whimsically but accurately that the universe was missing. Much of my poetry has tried to use the vagaries of quantum mechanics, that wall of probability that Einstein, it is said by many bad biographers, hurled himself against in pathos. Kenneth Koch once told a class that a painter should have a good title, like 'The Lost Golf Ball,' so that at the least one would be incited to look for something. My sister gave me packages of glowing stars in California, and the package had the extraordinary logo: 'Make your room a universe.' Some of my poems have appropriated lines from grammar textbooks and physics textbooks but transformed them, I would hope, by context. Much of the comical anguish of this poem came by the accident of losing it for a week or so and trying to find 'The Lost Golf Ball.' Though this is a love poem for Lindsay Stamm, I would dedicate it to Walter Eisenberg, chemistry professor at Weequahic High School and expert in golf. He suggested that poems of mine on subjects like sports might have more appeal than most of my others. At least one friend thought the title too silly for the long sequence it initiates. But I use it as an analogue of Mozart's dark divertimento (in E-flat). Comment on poetics: Recently I have been disturbed by reductive conservatives who call for regularity in metrics and minimalists still acting as if nonreferential poems will disclose possibilities. I try to make a polyrhythmic poetry, inspired by Elliott Carter's sense, as clarified by David Schiff, that music can be mechanical, rubato, free, or accelerating and the reverse. Perhaps it is a deficiency that poetry does not make explicit notation of its metrical palette. I see no reason to keep to the monochrome of much recent poetry—the gray of 'language' poetries or that of the old (lack of) criteria. I am a 'poetry' poet and in favor of maximalism."

KARL SHAPIRO was born in Baltimore, Maryland, in 1913. Before completing his formal education at Johns Hopkins University, he entered the United States Army and served in the South Pacific during World War II. *V-Letter* (1944) won the Pulitzer Prize in 1945; *Essay on Rime* (1945) was written while he was still on duty in the South Pacific. From 1950 until 1956, Shapiro was the editor of *Poetry*. In 1956 he joined the faculty of the University of Nebraska and became the editor of *Prairie Schooner*. His other books of poetry include *Poems of a Jew* (1958) and *Selected Poems* (1968).

Karl Shapiro writes: "Actually this poem ('Tennyson') is one of a pair. The other is 'Whitman' and will appear in *The American Scholar*. There was a strong literary flirtation between the two poets, which came to nothing."

CHARLES SIMIC was born in Yugoslavia in 1938. He was educated at the University of Chicago and at New York University. His most recent books are *Selected Poems 1963–1983* (Braziller, 1985), and *Unending Blues* (1986) and *The World Doesn't End* (1989), both from Harcourt Brace Jovanovich. He has published numerous books of translations of Yugoslav poetry as well as a book of essays and interviews titled *The Uncertain Certainty* (University of Michigan Press, 1985). Married and the father of two children, he teaches at the University of New Hampshire.

Simic read "The White Room" as the Phi Beta Kappa poem at Harvard University in 1988. He writes: " 'The White Room' is about the world with eyes open versus the world with eyes closed. Emily Dickinson is in it. I wrote it sitting by my window, listening to the trees, watching the empty road, and thinking of other trees and roads and solitudes."

LOUIS SIMPSON was born in Jamaica, British West Indies, in 1923. He emigrated to the United States at the age of seventeen, attended Columbia University, then served with the 101st Airborne Division on active duty in France, Holland, Belgium, and Germany. He is the author of ten books of poetry, including *At the End of the Open Road* (1963), which won the Pulitzer Prize. He recently published his *Collected Poems* (1988) and *Selected Prose* (1989), both from Paragon House. He has completed a book of new poems that is scheduled for publication in 1990, and is now working on a book of prose. He teaches at the State University of New York at Stony Brook, and lives in Setauket, New York.

Simpson writes: " 'The People Next Door' is written in free form, in a conversational style. This is typical of my way of writing. The content is also typical: it speaks about everyday life in the United States. The originality of the poem is that I do not look at that life from a distance but as one who shares it. I am happy to have written the poem because it expresses what I really think and feel."

W. D. SNODGRASS was born in Wilkinsburg, Pennsylvania, in 1926. He attended Geneva College and served in the Navy during World War II. *Heart's Needle*, his first book, won the Pulitzer Prize for poetry in 1960. He recently published his *Selected Poems 1957–1987* (SoHo Press, 1987). A collection of critical essays and lectures, *In Radical Pursuit* (Harper & Row), appeared in 1975. He is currently a professor of English at the University of Delaware.

Of "The Memory of Cock Robin Dwarfs W. D.," Snodgrass writes: "DeLoss McGraw and I have worked together collaboratively on a lot of poems and paintings. In this case the painting came first. It depicted the enormous head of a bird, which dwarfed the figure of a man. It reminded me of the beginning of Rilke's *Duino Elegies*—and also of Brahms's statement about Beethoven: 'You can't imagine how that man's footsteps echo behind us.' Beauty, and the memory of beauty, and trying to live up to it, is very terrifying."

GARY SNYDER was born in San Francisco in 1930. At Reed College in Portland, Oregon, he received an interdepartmental B.A. in literature and anthropology in 1951. In 1956 he went to Kyoto, Japan, to pursue studies in Far Eastern culture and Zen Buddhist texts. He stayed in Japan through 1968. Since 1970, he has been living in the northern Sierra Nevada on the edge of the Tahoe National Forest. He has been a member of the English department of the University of California at Davis, since 1985. Snyder has published fourteen books of poetry and prose. *Turtle Island* (New Directions, 1974) won the Pulitzer Prize for poetry in 1975.

ELIZABETH SPIRES was born in Lancaster, Ohio, in 1952 and was educated at Vassar College and Johns Hopkins University. Her most recent book is *Annonciade*, published by Viking Penguin in 1989. She is also the author of *Globe* (Wesleyan University Press, 1981) and *Swan's Island* (Henry Holt, 1985). She recently held the Amy Lowell Travelling Poetry Scholarship. Currently, she lives in Baltimore and teaches at Goucher College.

Spires writes: " 'Sunday Afternoon at Fulham Palace' was written at the beginning of a year's stay in London. Living in another country for the first time in my life made me feel, in a vague, inarticulate way, both more vulnerable and more aware of global interconnections. If a nuclear war were to happen, I was far from 'home' and safety. This probably was the unconscious psychic background for the specific occasion of the poem, an actual visit to Fulham Palace one Sunday afternoon. All of it 'really happened,' from the Fulham Band's overture, 'Those Magnificent Men in Their Flying Machines,' to the overheard remark of the little girl, 'I was thinking about what kind of anesthesia they'll give me when I have my first baby'!"

WILLIAM STAFFORD, retired from a long stint at Lewis and Clark College, lives in Oregon. He was born in 1914 in Hutchinson, Kansas. His main poetry collections have come along regularly from Harper & Row since the early 1960s; three are in print now, the first of which collects all material from earlier Harper & Row books: *Stories That Could Be True* (1977), *A Glass Face in the Rain*, (1982), and *An Oregon Message* (1987).

His other books include two in the University of Michigan series of poets on writing (*Writing the Australian Crawl*, 1978, and *You Must Revise Your Life*, 1987); *Down in My Heart* (an account of being a conscientious objector in World War II, first published in 1947 and currently in print from the Bench Press, which first republished the book in 1985); *Smoke's Way* (collected poems from small presses, published by Graywolf Press in 1978); and many smaller collections of poems from such companies as David Godine, the Perishable Press, Honeybrook Press, Copper Canyon, BOA, Alembic, and others.

Stafford writes: " 'Last Day,' first titled 'Last Day at Camp,' came drifting out of my daily practice while at the Centrum writers' conference up on Puget Sound. A mild rain blessed us on the last day of our conference, and we felt good about our time together and about the rain, so mild, so valedictory. I began to like what sprouted from my daily scribbling.

"The first quatrain settled, at first, into past tense; and in fact my documentary copy (the typed version I keep, and on which I sometimes continue to scribble nudges at the text) has my penned changes to present tense. My pen continues to hover at the first verb in the second quatrain, but so far I have gone with the impulse to give a shadowy touch of realization that the people at the camp had brought gifts to each other when they came, gifts of themselves. (Too faint a touch? I live by such shadowy presences of local influences from the time when I am writing first drafts.) Of course there were innumerable choices and waverings as I teased the poem out of its hiding place in the world and in my consciousness. One such choice still reveals itself in typed versus penned version, the idea of using either 'another time' or 'a better time' at the end."

GEORGE STARBUCK, born in 1931, used to teach at Boston University. A recording of him reading is available from Watershed, Washington, D.C. His fifth book, *The Argot Merchant Disaster: New and Selected Poems* (Atlantic Monthly Press, 1982), won the 1983 Lenore Marshall Prize. Two tiny books from Bits Press appeared in 1986: *Space-Saver Sonnets* and *Richard the Third in a Fourth of a Second.*

Of "Reading the Facts about Frost in *The Norton Anthology*," Starbuck writes: "Must I comment on the poem?

"A poem about poetry is bad enough. A poem about blather about poets must be worse. And then to commit blather about *that*?? . . .

"I'll seek safety in prosody-talk.

"The flat five-by-five syllabic stanza proved useful: farthest thing from Frost's own grand iambic. Frost played safari-guide among a whole Serengheti of prosodic life-forms, played host to the whole unbroken iambic lineage. As if simple iambic had the generative, diversifying power of simple DNA. He cast his eye on New Hampshire and the woods were full of them: wizard sentences, feral, ears-up, ready to bolt, to lope and pronk, to breathe easy again in groups and safely graze. And no ditsy guest better approach pushing some wheeled submission of taxidermic approximations.

"So I stole a form from altogether elsewhere. From Donald Hall as a matter of fact, who suddenly did 5-by syllabics in about 1960, to great effect."

PATRICIA STORACE was born in Chicago and grew up in Mobile, Alabama. Her first book, *Heredity*, won the first Barnard New

Women Poets Prize and was published by Beacon Press in 1987. She is an assistant editor at *The New York Review of Books* and poetry editor of *The Paris Review*.

Storace writes: " 'Movie' began with a boring image of the banks of candles in front of saints' statues in Catholic churches. I did not want part of my mind trapped in some church where it had no business, and traced the association until I realized that it was the faces and bodies of people in movies that seemed to me like candles. Seen both in front of and above you, these filmed people are light, with the same poignance of candlelight in seeming to be both real and remembered at once. Part of the power of movie images is that they make you feel as if you are not only seeing them, but remembering them.

"Technically, I hoped to write a poem without event or anecdote, in which the words themselves would be dreamlike, as with *again* in the last line, repeated to the point where it stops being a word and becomes a feeling. I hope this doesn't sound like self-important mumbo-jumbo. If so, I join Cary Grant/C. K. Dexter Haven (*The Philadelphia Story*) in saying, 'Ain't it awful?' "

MARK STRAND was born on Prince Edward Island, Canada, in 1934. He was educated at Yale and at the University of Iowa. He currently teaches in the creative writing program at the University of Utah. He is the author of six books of poems, including *The Story of Our Lives* (1973), *The Late Hour* (1978) and *Selected Poems* (1980), all published by Atheneum. In 1990, Knopf will bring out a new collection of his poems. His most recent book is *William Bailey* (Abrams, 1986), a study of the painter.

Of "Reading in Place," Strand writes: "I have nothing to say about the poem that the poem doesn't say about itself, except, perhaps, that 'Where, where in Heaven am I?' comes from Robert Frost's poem 'Lost in Heaven.' "

ELEANOR ROSS TAYLOR was born in North Carolina in 1920. She graduated from the Women's College of the University of North Carolina at Greensboro in 1940. In 1943 she married the writer Peter Taylor. Her first book of poems, *Wilderness of Ladies*, was published by McDowell, Obolensky in 1960. It was followed by

Welcome Eumenides (Braziller, 1972) and *New and Selected Poems* (Stuart Wright, 1986). She is now living in Gainesville, Florida, but maintains ties with her native North Carolina and with Virginia.

JEAN VALENTINE was born in Chicago and raised mostly in New York City and Boston. Her first book, *Dream Barker*, was published in the Yale Series of Younger Poets in 1964. She has published five collections since, most recently *Home. Deep. Blue: New and Selected Poems* (Alice James Books, 1989). She has received fellowships from the Guggenheim Foundation and the Bunting Institute. She teaches at Sarah Lawrence College and at the West Side Y and lives in New York City.

RICHARD WILBUR was born in New York City in 1921. World War II took him to Cassino, Anzio, and the Siegfried Line. After the war he studied at Harvard, then taught there and at Wellesley and Wesleyan. He has translated Molière's *The Misanthrope* and *Tartuffe* and Racine's *Phaedra*. His *New and Collected Poems*, published by Harcourt Brace Jovanovich in 1988, won the *Los Angeles Times* Poetry Prize. In 1987–88, he served as the nation's second official poet laureate, succeeding Robert Penn Warren.

Of "Lying," Richard Wilbur has written that he chose blank verse ("the most flexible of our meters, and the best in which to build large verse-masses") and that the poem is addressed to "You" ("perhaps because everybody is something of a poet"). He adds: "When I first showed 'Lying' to my wife, who is always the first and best reader of my poems, she said, 'Well, you've finally done it; you've managed to write a poem that's incomprehensible from beginning to end.' Then, reading it again, she came to find it, considered as a statement, quite forthright. It seems that 'Lying' is the sort of poem which ought first to be heard or read without any distracting anxiety to catch all of its connections and local effects, and that it then asks to be absorbed in several readings or hearings. I make no apology for that: some of the poetry written these days has the relaxed transparency of talk, and would not profit by being mulled over, but much is of the concentrated kind which closes with an implicit *da capo*. Provided it's any good, a poem which took months to write deserves an ungrudging quarter hour from the reader.

"I'm reluctant to expound the obvious, saying for instance that there are 'lies' or fictions which are ways of telling the truth, and that the poem ends with three fictions having one burden. What I would most respond to, in conversation with an interested reader, would be noticings or questionings of details: the use of birds throughout, and of the word *shrug* for the hovering of an unreal grackle; the echo of Job, and its intended evocation of a whole passage; the water-figure, strange but not untrue, in which the idea of 'nothing' is dismissed; the transformation of the *black mist* into a rainbow; the perching of the catbird on a mock-orange spray; the vitrification of a river, beginning with 'glazes' and ending with 'cullet.' But the fact is that the details are too many for me to worry them in this space; what we have here, I figure, is a baroque poem, in the sense that it is a busy and intricate contraption which issues in plainness."

ALAN WILLIAMSON was born in 1944 and grew up in Chicago, with summers in California. His books of poetry are *Presence* (1983) and *The Muse of Distance* (1988), both from Knopf. He has also written two books of criticism, *Pity the Monsters: The Political Vision of Robert Lowell* (Yale University Press, 1974) and *Introspection and Contemporary Poetry* (Harvard University Press, 1984). He teaches at the University of California at Davis.

Of "The Muse of Distance," Williamson writes: "I have always loved the many-voiced American long poems—*The Bridge, Paterson*—but this is the nearest I have ever come to writing one. Much of it started out as an unsuccessful short story, then wrote itself over into meter and somehow felt freer. So much time, and so much of my private history, went into it that I don't know what to say further. I've been pleased that many of its hearers have found it familiar, and 'American.' "

JAY WRIGHT's books include his *Selected Poems*, edited by Robert B. Stepto with an afterword by Harold Bloom (Princeton University Press, 1987), and *Elaine's Book* (University Press of Virginia, 1988). He lives in New Hampshire.

MAGAZINES WHERE THE POEMS
WERE FIRST PUBLISHED

American Poetry Review, eds. David Bonanno, Stephen Berg, and Arthur Vogelsang. Temple University Center City, 1616 Walnut St., Room 405, Philadelphia, Pa. 19103

The Atlantic Monthly, poetry ed. Peter Davison. 8 Arlington Street, Boston, Mass. 02116

Boulevard, ed. Richard Burgin. 2400 Chestnut Street, #3301, Philadelphia, Pa. 19103

Epoch, ed. Cecil Giscombe. 251 Goldwin Smith Hall, Cornell University, Ithaca, N.Y. 14853

Exquisite Corpse, ed. Andrei Codrescu. Culture Shock Foundation, English Department, Louisiana State University, Baton Rouge, La. 70803

The Georgia Review, ed. Stanley Lindberg. University of Georgia, Athens, Ga. 30602

The Gettysburg Review, ed. Peter Stitt. Gettysburg College, Gettysburg, Pa. 17325

Grand Street, ed. Ben Sonnenberg. 50 Riverside Drive, New York, N.Y. 10024

Green Mountains Review, poetry ed. Neil Shepard. Johnson State College, Department of English, Johnson, Vt. 05656

Harvard Magazine, poetry ed. Donald Hall. 7 Ware Street, Cambridge, Mass. 02138

The Hudson Review, eds. Paula Deitz and Frederick Morgan. 684 Park Avenue, New York, N.Y. 10021

The Iowa Review, ed. David Hamilton. 308 EPB, University of Iowa, Iowa City, Iowa, 52242

Longhouse. Green River Stage, Brattleboro, Vt. 05301

Michigan Quarterly Review, ed. Laurence Goldstein. University of Michigan, 3032 Rackham Building, Ann Arbor, Mich. 48109-1070

Mudfish, ed. Jill Hoffman. Box Turtle Press/Attitude Art Inc. 184 Franklin Street, New York, N.Y. 10013

New American Writing, eds. Maxine Chernoff and Paul Hoover. 2920 West Pratt, Chicago, Ill. 60645

The New Criterion, poetry ed. Robert Richman. 850 Seventh Avenue, New York, N.Y. 10019

The New York Review of Books, eds. Barbara Epstein and Robert Silvers. 250 West 57th Street, New York, N.Y. 10107

The New Yorker, poetry ed. Alice Quinn. 25 West 43rd Street, New York, N.Y. 10036

O.blek, eds. Peter Gizzi and Connell McGrath. Box 836, Stockbridge, Mass. 01262

The Ohio Review, ed. Wayne Dodd. Ohio University, 320 Ellis Hall, Athens, Ohio 45701-2979

The Paris Review, poetry ed. Patricia Storace. 541 East 72nd Street, New York, N.Y. 10021

Partisan Review, ed. William Phillips. Boston University, 141 Bay State Road, Boston, Mass. 02215

Poetry, ed. Joseph Parisi. 60 West Walton Street, Chicago, Ill. 60610

Raritan, ed. Richard Poirier. Rutgers University, 165 College Avenue, New Brunswick, N.J. 08903

The Reaper, eds. Mark Jarman and Robert McDowell. Story Line Press, 403 Continental Street, Santa Cruz, Calif. 95060

Seneca Review, ed. Deborah Tall. Hobart and William Smith Colleges, Geneva, N.Y. 14456-3397

Shenandoah, ed. Dabney Stuart. The Washington and Lee University Review, Box 722, Lexington, Va. 24450

Sulfur, ed. Clayton Eshleman. English Department, Eastern Michigan University, Ypsilanti, Mich. 48197

Times Literary Supplement, literary ed. Alan Jenkins. Priory House, St. John's Lane, London EC1M 4BX, England

Western Humanities Review, ed. Barry Weller. 341 Orson Spenser Hall, University of Utah, Salt Lake City, Utah 84112

Willow Springs. Eastern Washington University, P.U.B., Box 1063, MS-1, Cheney, Wash. 99004

Witness, ed. Peter Stine. 31000 Northwestern Highway, Suite 200, Farmington Hills, Mich. 48018

The Yale Review, poetry ed. J. D. McClatchy. P.O. Box 1902A Yale Station, New Haven, Conn. 06520

ACKNOWLEDGMENTS

Grateful acknowledgment is made to the publications from which the poems in this volume were chosen. Unless specifically noted otherwise, copyright of the poems is held by the individual poets.

A. R. Ammons: "Anxiety's Prosody" first appeared in *Poetry*, October 1988. Copyright © 1988 by the Modern Poetry Association. Reprinted by permission of the poet and the editor of *Poetry*.

John Ashbery: "Meanwhile . . ." first appeared in *Mudfish* #3. Reprinted by permission.

Beth Bentley: "Northern Idylls" appeared originally in *The Gettysburg Review*, vol. I., no. 4, 1988. Reprinted by permission.

Elizabeth Bishop: "It is marvellous . . ." was first published in *American Poetry Review*, vol. 17, #1. Copyright © 1988 by Alice Helen Methfessel. Reprinted by permission of Farrar, Straus & Giroux, Inc. Lorrie Goldensohn's comments appeared in *American Poetry Review*. Reprinted by permission.

Robert Bly: "My Father at 85" appeared in *Common Ground, A Gathering of Poets from the 1986 Marshall Festival*, edited by Mark Vinz and Thom Tammaro. Copyright © 1988 by Dacotah Territory Press. Reprinted by permission of the poet and the publisher.

Catherine Bowman: "Twins of a Gazelle Which Feed Among the Lilies" first appeared in *The Paris Review*. Reprinted by permission.

George Bradley: "Of the Knowledge of Good and Evil" appeared originally in *The New Yorker*. Copyright © 1988 by George Bradley. Reprinted by permission.

David Budbill: "What I Heard at the Discount Department Store" appeared in *Longhouse*. Reprinted by permission of the poet.

Michael Burkard: "Hotel Tropicana" was first published in *Epoch* (37:1). Reprinted by permission of the poet and the editor of *Epoch*.

Amy Clampitt: "A Minor Tremor" appeared originally in *Boulevard*. Reprinted by permission.

Tom Clark: "For Robert Duncan" appeared originally in *Exquisite Corpse*. Reprinted by permission.

Clark Coolidge: "Paris . . ." appeared originally in *O.blēk*. Reprinted by permission of the poet.

Douglas Crase: "True Solar Holiday" appeared originally in *The Yale Review*. Reprinted by permission of the poet.

Robert Creeley: "Age" appeared under the title "Talking of Age" in *New American Writing*, #3. Reprinted by permission.

in *Epoch* (37:2). Reprinted by permission of the poet and the editor of *Epoch*.

Sharon Olds: "The Wellspring" was first published in *American Poetry Review*, vol. 17, no. 3. Reprinted by permission.

Mary Oliver: "Some Questions You Might Ask" first appeared in *Harvard Magazine*. Reprinted by permission.

Steve Orlen: "The Bridge of Sighs" first appeared in *The Atlantic Monthly*. Reprinted by permission of the poet.

Michael Palmer: "Sun" from *Sun* by Michael Palmer (North Point Press, 1988). Copyright © 1988 by Michael Palmer. Reprinted by permission of North Point Press.

Bob Perelman: "Movie" from *Captive Audience* by Bob Perelman (The Figures, 1988). Copyright © 1988 by Bob Perelman. Reprinted by permission of the poet and the publisher.

Robert Pinsky: "At Pleasure Bay" first appeared in *Raritan*. Reprinted by permission of the poet and the editors of *Raritan*.

Anna Rabinowitz: "Sappho Comments on an Exhibition of Expressionist Landscapes" first appeared in *Sulfur*. Reprinted by permission of the poet.

Mark Rudman: "The Shoebox" first appeared in *The Paris Review*. Reprinted by permission.

David St. John: "Broken Gauges" appeared originally in *Green Mountains Review*, vol. 2, no. 1. Reprinted by permission of the poet.

Yvonne Sapia: "Valentino's Hair" from *Valentino's Hair* by Yvonne Sapia. Copyright © 1987 by Yvonne Sapia. Reprinted with the permission of Northeastern University Press. The poem appeared in *The Reaper* in 1988.

Lynda Schraufnagel: "Trappings" first appeared in *Shenandoah*, vol. 37, no. 4 (1987). Copyright © 1987 by Washington and Lee University. Reprinted from *Shenandoah* with the permission of the editor.

David Shapiro: "The Lost Golf Ball" from *House (Blown Apart)* by David Shapiro (Overlook, 1988). Copyright © 1988 by David Shapiro. Reprinted by permission.

Karl Shapiro: "Tennyson" appeared originally in *The New Yorker*. Copyright © 1988 by Karl Shapiro. Reprinted by permission.

Charles Simic: "The White Room" first appeared in *Western Humanities Review*, vol. 41, no. 4 (Winter 1988). Reprinted by permission. Mr. Simic read "The White Room" as the Phi Beta Kappa poem at Harvard University in 1988.

Louis Simpson: "The People Next Door" first appeared in *Poetry*, May 1988. Copyright © 1988 by The Modern Poetry Association. Reprinted by permission of the poet and the editor of *Poetry*.

W. D. Snodgrass: "The Memory of Cock Robin Dwarfs W. D." first appeared in *Michigan Quarterly Review*. Reprinted by permission.